# BIG FISH IN
# FOREIGN WATERS

by

Tony Davies-Patrick
Leon Hoogendijk

First published in 1991 by
Paisley-Wilde Publishing Ltd.
1 Grosvenor Square,
Sheffield S2 4MS

British Library Cataloguing in Publication Data

Tony Davies-Patrick, Leon Hoogendijk
Big Fish in Foreign Waters
1. Carp. Angling
I. Title
799.1'752

ISBN 1 871700 507

❀❀❀❀❀❀❀

Produced, Typeset and Published by
Paisley-Wilde Publishing Ltd.

Printed by
Gibbons Barford Print Ltd.

# Acknowledgements

The authors wish to thank the following for their contributions to this book:

RINI GROOTHUIS, JENS BURSELL, DIDIER COTTIN,
JOHNNY JENSEN and INGAR CHRISTOPHER SOLBERG
for their written and photographic contributions.

BRAM GROOTHUIS, OLE B. NIELSON, THOMAS VEDEL,
HEINZ JAGUSCH, MADS KRISTOFFERSON,
JEAN-PIERRE POULALIER, RUNE JOHANSEN, PETE KNIGHT,
INGAR HEUM, Mr. BERT, FRANK JENSEN, TOME OLE HOLTH,
PETER RUNNPURGE, CLAUS MILKEREIT, THIERRY DUBAIL,
ZELKO KRALJ, KENTH ESBENSEN and JENS PLOUG HANSEN
for their help with photographs and information.

and all the people and friends we've met on our travels in search of
"Big Fish in Foreign Waters".

I dedicate this book to my daughter, Amber

Other titles published by
Paisley-Wilde Publishing Ltd


CARPWORLD MAGAZINE

BIG FISH WORLD MAGAZINE

CARP SEASON – *Tim Paisley*

MYWATER – *Elliott Symak*

CARP IN FOCUS – *Photographic Compilation*

CARPWORLD YEARBOOK – *Kevin Clifford, Julian Cundiff*


*Carp in Depth Series*

TACKLE & TACTICS – *Ken Townley*

CARP BAITS – *Tim Paisley, Bill Cottam*

RIGS AND END TACKLE – *Alan Tomkins*

FLOATER FISHING – *Chris Ball, Brian Skoyles*

CARP WATERS – *Julian Cundiff*

WINTER CARPING – *Derek Stritton*

PARTICLE BAITS – *Paul Gummer, Dickie Caldwell*

THE CARP – *Kevin Clifford, Tim Paisley*


*Videos*

CARP BAITS – THE VIDEO – *Tim Paisley and Friends*

BIRCH GROVE SESSION – PARTS 1 & 2 – *Tim Paisley and John Lilley*

# Contents

Tony Davies-Patrick

# Introduction

Ever since I first spent countless hours in the large bookshops and libraries of Bristol in a fruitless search for detailed information on freshwater fishing abroad, I have known that a real gap has needed to be filled in fishing literature. The amazing response from readers around Europe to the various articles I have written on fishing abroad, requesting further information, has strengthened that belief.

I have tried to cram as much information as possible into the chapters that follow, cover almost all the best waters and mention the most predominate species and maximum weights that they can achieve in each particular lake, river or canal. The information dwells heavily on the most popular species: the reason for including a chapter on the mighty Mahseer of India, is because of its increasing popularity amongst holiday anglers and because it must rate as **the** freshwater fish to have on the end of the line. Johnny Jensen takes us out of our armchairs and into the jungle to tackle some massive Indian "queens of the river".

The carp is probably the most popular fish in Europe and the interest in European carp waters has grown like wild-fire in recent years. It is for this reason that the book slants heavily on carp fishing.

To add spice to a reference and information book for anglers in search of foreign waters, we have included guest chapters, and interviews from two very successful carp anglers in Europe, namely, Didier Cottin from France and Jens Bursell from Denmark.

There is an amazing call for detailed information on carp fishing in France and Holland, and the book needed an angler of Leon Hoogèndijk's calibre to fill that gap. Leon has written a large chunk of this book and his first hand accounts of French and Dutch carp fishing make fascinating reading.

Belgium has been overlooked in the past by many canal carp anglers in their rush to get to France or Holland. Belgium's canals needed a special type of angler to tap their enormous potential - a special type of angler like Bram Groothuis - and it needed a special type of writer to transfer Bram's successes onto paper; a respected carp angler, one who was closest to Bram's own feelings - none other than Rini Groothuis, his brother, and I can think of no one who could have written it better.

To include all the addresses of places to obtain licences, prices, telephone numbers etc., was quite unnecessary and would have filled half of the pages of this book. Licences for the majority of waters mentioned in this book can be obtained from any of the Tourist Offices situated in all the major towns, or in club houses, hotels, petrol stations and tackle shops close to the waters. In some countries, such as Germany and France, large affiliated organisations cover many different waters on one ticket. In a few cases, the landowner's permission is needed. The strict examinations for German fishermen does not apply to visitors from foreign countries whilst on holiday. Some countries (or areas of those countries) have different close seasons for certain fish; apply to the Tourist Office of the area you are about to go to if you are in any doubt.

In the Norwegian chapter, very precise details of location and fish stocks, access, etc., have been given, as this is the first time that details of coarse fishing in Norway have ever been published. This chapter was compiled by Ingar Christopher Solberg, Rune Johansen, Pete Knight, Ingar Heum and Tom Ole Holth.

Remember that weights given in the 'tour' chapters are 'maximum' weights known in these waters, and that only a few fish in the natural 'pyramid' can reach these maximum weights.

Don't expect too much from your holiday on a foreign water. Many anglers are going abroad in the belief that they've **got** to catch a huge fish otherwise the trip will be a failure. This is especially happening in France. How many hours, how many baits, how much time and effort do you actually put into your own waters each year? And how many 'big' fish do you actually manage to land after all that effort? Yet some of you expect to visit an unknown water for a few days or a few weeks, with no previous knowledge of how the water 'ticks', to pop in at any time of the year and land almost every fish that swims! "I've been fishing this lake all week and it's supposed to hold 40's yet I haven't seen anything like that weight caught yet!" You might think that would be a stupid remark if you were standing on the banks of Redmire or the Snake Pit - yet some people stand on the banks of thousands of acres of water and say those very words after their first short visit!

Take, for example, the Lake Castelnau in France. This lake's top weight for carp is 40lb+, yet the average fish you're likely to catch is 5-15lb! Yes, there are good twenties, thirties, and some beautiful, long 40lb+ commons in the water, and if you get everything right and arrive at the right time of year, with luck, you might catch one. But these lucky few are a drop in the ocean compared to the thousands of anglers who flock to this type of water every year.

Plan your holiday with enjoyment in mind and arrive home refreshed and happy, whether you've landed your first 40lb common, 20lb zander, 20lb trout, 100lb catfish etc., or whether you've spent the whole holiday in the pouring rain watching glued indicators or static swingtips: there's always next year!

Life's too short to worry whilst on holiday; after all, the doctor said that you needed a 'break' from all that worry! Chuck those rods in the back of the car, or the telescopic rod in the rucksack and go out there and enjoy life!

The best of luck to all of you for the future.

Tony Davies-Patrick

# About Leon

Hello, my name is Leon Hoogendijk and I wouldn't be at all surprised if you've never heard of me before, so let me introduce myself to you in a few words.

I was born in 1964, in a little village called Oud-Verlaat in the west of Holland. I caught my very first carp at the age of 6 on a bamboo rod, whilst fishing for roach with breadflake. It weighed one pound!

Until my 10th birthday, I caught quite a lot of these mini carp on my old bamboo rod, then I got my first ringed rod and reel, a massive glass spinning rod of 6ft. and a reel which was the cheapest that existed in that period. With that combination I caught all kinds of species, pike, perch, tench, big roach (over 18 inches long!) and an eel. The eel, I caught accidentally on a worm while fishing for perch and, at ten years old, I was afraid of eels! I remember running a mile with my rod up in the air and the eel flying behind me. Back at home I threw the rod and eel in the garden and told my father to unhook this snaky monster for me. It was the last time that I fished for perch with worms!

I also caught a lot of small carp (up to 4lb) on my cheap rod, fishing with potatoes in the 'polders' of my region, and these carp became my favourite species.

At the age of 13 I bought my first glass carp rod and a Shakespeare 2200 reel with the money I had earned working for a farmer during the school holidays.

A year later I moved to another village called Krimpen aan de Yssel (also in west Holland). Here I caught my first 'big' carp, a $17\frac{1}{2}$lb leather (big for me, at the time). I had this fish in the small park water (2 acres) next to my home. After this capture, carp fishing really became my passion. I fished the little pool for three years and caught almost all the fish, about 80 different carp, most of them commons, up to 25lb on paste baits and floating crusts, using classic methods. Then, in a terrible cold winter, the shallow pool was iced up for over ten weeks and almost all the carp died!

The next year I moved to other waters and met other carp anglers, some of whom became very close friends. We were all very competitive at the time, but this made us learn quickly. In fact, I became so competitive that for a certain period in my life the hobby became an obsession. I know that this is wrong, but I'm glad to have gone through that period because it was during that time that I learned most about carp and carp fishing.

In the following years I fished bigger waters for bigger carp. I wanted twenties, then upper twenties and finally thirties.

At the age of 23, I moved to France and married a French lady. This was also the beginning of a new chapter about mysterious virgin waters, really huge lakes and beautiful rivers holding even bigger carp! Yes, I love carp! It's an essential part of my life; something I can't explain, but some of you will know what I mean.

I never had the intention of writing for a book because I don't consider myself a top carp angler, although I have caught over 1,000 carp now; over 200 twenties and many thirties up to over 50lb. I know of people who have done a lot better than me, but they don't write about their catches! However, when Tony asked me to write for a book I thought I might as well give it a try and write some chapters. I hope you enjoy them.

Leon Hoogendijk

# Fish Names in Europe

Abbreviations:    E = English; L = Latin; D = Danish; N = Norway; S = Sweden; G = German; SP = Spanish; Y = Yugoslav (Serbo-Croat); F = French; FI = Finnish; I = Italian; H = Holland.


**E: ASP** — L: Aspius Aspius; D: Asp; N: Asp; S: Asp; G: Rapfen; Y: Bolen; F: Aspe; FI Toutain.

**E: BARBEL** — L: Barbus Barbus; D: Flodbarbe; S: Flodbarb; G: Barbe; SP: Barbo (comizo); Y: Mrena; I: Barbo; H: Barbeel; F: Barbeau.

**E: BREAM** — L: Abramis Brama; D: Brasen; N: Brase; S: Braxen; G: Brassen; Y: Plośćić; F: Bréme, FI: Lahna; H: Brasem.

**E: BLACK BASS** — L: Micropterus Salmonides/Dolomica; D: Blackbass; S: Blackbass; G: Forellenbarsch; Y: Ostracka; F: Blackbass; FI: Pikkubassi; I: Percio Trota.

**E: BURBOT** — L: Lota Lota; D: Ferskvandskvabbe/Knude; N: Lake; S: Lake; G: Rutte; Y: Menek/Manic; F: Lote; FI: Made; I: Bottarice; H: Kwabaal.

**E: CARP** — L: Cyprinus Carpio; D: Karpe; N: Karpe; S: Karp; G: Karpfen; SP: Carpa; Y: Krap/Saran; FI: Karpii, I: Carpa; H: Karper.

**E: CATFISH** — L: Silurus Glanis; D: Malle; N: Malle; S: Mal; G: Wels; SP: Silura; Y: Som; F: Silure; FI: Monni; I: Siluro; H: Meerval.

**E: CHAR/ARCTIC CHAR** — L: Salvenius Alpinus; D: Fjeldørred; N: Røyr; S: Röding; G: Saibling; Y: Jerzerska zialovcica; F: Omble Chevalier; FI: Nieriä; I: Cavalliere.

**E: CHUB** — L: Leuciscus cephalus; D: Døbel; N: Stamm; S: Färna; G: Döbel, SP: Cacho; Y: Kjen; F: Chevesne; FI: Turpa; I: Cavedano; H: Meun.

**E: CRUCIAN CARP** — L: Carassius carassius; D: Karusse; N: Karudse; S: Ruda; G: Karauche; SP: Carpin; Y: Karal; F: Carassin; FI: Ruutana.

**E: DANUBE SALMON** — L: Hucho Hucho; D: Donoulaks; N: Donoulaks, S: Donoulax; G: Huchen; Y: Mladica/Sulec; F: Saumon huch/Huchon; FI: Tonavan; I: Salmone del Danubio; H: Donauzalm.

**E: EEL** — L: Anguilla Anguilla; D: ÅI; N: ÅI; S: ÅI; G: Aal; SP: Anguila; Y: Jegulja; F: Anguille; FI: Ankerias/Airokas; I: Anguilla; H: Paling.

**E: GRAYLING** — D: Stalling; N: Harr; S: Harr; G: Äsche; Y: Lipljen/Lipan; F: Ombre; FI: Harjus; I: Temulo; H: Vlagsalm; L: Thymallus thymallus.

**E: IDE** — L: Leuciscus Idus; D: Rimte; N: Vederbuk; S: Id; G: Aland; Y: Jez; F: Ide; FI: Saynas; H: Winde.

**E: PERCH** — L: Perca Fluviatilis; D: Aborre; N: Abbore; S: Abbore; G: Barsche; SP: Perca; Y: Grgeć, F: Perche; FI: Abon; I: Perca; H: Baars.

**E: PIKE** — L: Esox Lucius; D: Gedde; N: Gedda; S: Gadda; G: Hecht; SP: Lucio; Y: Stuka; F: Brochet; I: Luccio; H: Snoek.

**E: POWAN/WHITEFISH** — L: Corogenus Lavaretus, D: Helt; N: Sik; G: Maräne, Y: Marena velka, F: Laveret/Corégone, FI: Siika/Miukku, S: Sik.

**E: ROACH** — L: Rutilus rutilus; D: Skalle; N: Mort; S: Mört; G: Plötze; Y: Brodorka/Rdeceoka; F: Gardon; FI: Särki; H: Blankvoorn.

**E: RUDD** — L: Scardinius Erythropthalmus; D: Rudskalle; N: Sørv; S: Sarv; D: Rotfeder; Y: Crvenderka/Rdeceperca; F: Rotengle; I: Scardola; H: Ruisvoorn.

**E: SALMON** — L: Salmo Salar; D: Laks; N: Laks; S: Lax; G: Lacks; SP: Salmon; Y: Losos; F: Saumon; FI: Lohi; I: Salmone; H: Zalm.

**E: TENCH** — L: Tinca tinca; D: Suder; N: Suter; S: Sutare; G: Schlie; SP: Tenca; Y: Linjak/Ling; F: Tanche; FI: Suutari; I: Tinca; H: Zeelt.

**E: BROWN TROUT** — L: Salmo Trutta; D: Bækørred; N: Bekkørret; S: Bäcköring; G: Bachforelle; Y: Pastrimka; F: Truite; FI: Purolohi; I: Trotta; H: Beekforel.

**E: LAKE TROUT** - brown — L: Salmo Trutta-lacustris; D: Sø-ørred; N: Innsjø-ørret; S: Insjööring; G: Seeforelle; SP: Trutta; Y: Pastrva; F: Truite de lac; FI: Jarvilohi.

**E: SEA TROUT** — L: Salmo Trutta; D: Havørred; N: Sjø-ørret; S: Havsöring; D: Meerforelle; SP: Trutta marina; F: Truite de mer; FI: Meritaimen; I: Trota di lago.

**E: LAKE TROUT** - American — L: Salvnius Namaycush; D: Am. Søørred; N: Am. Sjöörret, F: Touladi; S: Kanadaröding; FI: Harmaanieriä; SP: Trutta lacustre.

**E: RAINBOW TROUT** — L: Salmo Gairdneri; D: Regnbueørred; N: Regnbueørret, S: Regnbåge; G: Regenbogenforelle; SP: Trucha arco-iris; Y: Kalifornisjka pastrmka; F: Truite arc-en-ciel; FI: Sateenkaa-virautu; H: Regenboogforell; I: Trota Iridia.

**E: ZANDER** — L: Stizostedion Lucioperka; D: Sandart; N: Gjors; S: Gös; G: Zander; F: Sandre; Y: Smudj; H: Sanner; FI Korka.

# Tackling Foreign Waters

Many of you reading this book will never have ventured onto foreign soil and the closest you've got to a foreign fish is maybe the last time that you visited the Chinese restaurant. This chapter sets out to explain the pitfalls that plague first trips and the best way of organising your future trips.

Obviously everyone is not a true adventurer and many people prefer the organised trips that are slowly becoming available, such as the Cassien coach trips and Anglers World Holidays, or with semi adventurous organised trips such as those offered by Geoff Shaw to France (tel. 0268 690844) and Tim Meadows of Anglers Abroad (tel. 0226 751704) to the Spanish islands.

Dave Plummer is now taking anglers on 7 day guided trips to the Canaries, which includes hotel accommodation at the Fina El Oso. The hotel provides many facilities and lies very close to Lake Chira, the home of many big carp between 20-40lb with some reaching 50lb+.

Flights depart 4th May 91; 1st June 91; 5th October 91. Prices start from £499 and include 7 days' fishing (and on hand help and advice from Dave), licences, accommodation, half board, flights and transfers.

For further information, contact Global Sportfishing, Tel. 0733 243206 or Norwich Angling Centre, Tel. 0603 400757.

All of these organised trips can offer wonderful holidays with some security, but even the supposedly organised trips can sometimes take the first time travellers unaware. Take for example the guy who phoned me after a disastrous trip to the Spanish islands, due not to the fact of bad fishing, but because of the harshly isolated areas where some of the lakes are located. Dragging the wife and kids over moon-type terrain in oven hot, blistering sunshine was not his idea of fun and ruined the complete holiday. This was an example of just how one small, but important, factor (that of ease of access) can affect your trip drastically.

Before you plan your trip, make sure that you understand how adventurous you intend to be and whether you want to travel alone or with the family. Obviously, if you intend to take the wife and kids along, you will have to plan accordingly. Pick a water that doesn't entail having to walk miles over barren rocks in high heels, or through stinking, mosquito-infested swamps, to get to! Choose an area close to shops, amusement centres, play areas or the beach. Try to choose a hotel, pension or campsite that is situated on, or close to, the water, and don't forget to find out what facilities the campsites offer. Some campsites are **very** basic, e.g. one cold water tap and a hole in the ground for a toilet, and some campsites wouldn't be out of place alongside the Savoy hotel, with everything from washing machines and video rooms to restaurants and night clubs - such as along the shores of the large south German lakes for example.

Write to the tourist office of the country that you intend to visit, or that country's Embassy in London, and they will be glad to send you leaflets on all available campsites, facilities, prices etc.

For those of you who are unsure of the exact areas you intend to fish, or who want to tour around different parts of the country, I would suggest that you spend ten minutes in the Tourist offices which are situated at all the passport control/ border crossings. Most of these will provide you with information on campsites and other accommodation etc., throughout the country.

Your mode of travel can count a great deal to the type of waters you can visit and the tackle you can carry. If you have a car or van, you can carry plenty of gear and bait and have the added advantage of being able to visit a number of waters with ease, which can be important if the first lake that you fish happens to be 'off' the feed. A motorbike is also good transport and a surprising amount of gear can be carried. Rods need to be strapped to the side of motorbikes and can get in the way at times; this is where telescopic rods score.

The big problem with telescopic rods is that there are very few around that are good quality. One particular telescopic rod that I bought from Walkers of Trowell and had strengthened by cutting a few inches off the top and adding a new Fuji top eye (on the kind advice from Shaun Harrison), worked well for many years.

The four piece carp rod designed by Rod Hutchinson and sold by Catchum is probably the best bet, but I would also prefer to see a lighter rod in the $1\frac{1}{2}$-2lb range on offer. After all, if you're travelling light you will probably carry only one or two rods and this will mean fishing for chub, bream, barbel, tench etc., with the same rod as you use for carp/cats/pike/mahseer, and a $1\frac{1}{2}$-$1\frac{3}{4}$lb is ideal. Obviously, if you intend to fish only for one particular species, then a more specialised rod can be taken. DAM Tackle have now made a 'suitcase' style, telescopic rod available and this is well worth investigating. Check with other manufacturers to see what they can offer for the travelling angler.

If you intend to travel by foot or local transport (bus, train, hitchhiking), make sure that you are well prepared before you set off. A good quality rucksack and walking boots are essential - make sure that you wear new boots 'in' before you set off! Try to take the minimum of equipment and when you've filled the rucksack, open it again and chuck out some more! Walking over mountainous terrain can be great fun and some of the best and most beautiful waters can only be seen this way. In the mountains a light telescopic is ideal, plus one reel, a bag of assorted end tackle and spares for the reel. Choose a well designed lightweight tent and always carry the correct clothing for unexpected weather conditions.

Travelling without your own transport means that you will have to rely on local food stores for bait if you wish to fish for any length of time. 10,000 boilies stuffed into your rucksack doesn't leave much space for anything else! Most large supermarkets contain a good range of possible baits to use for many different species. Be warned though that in countries such as Yugoslavia or Turkey the shelves can be very bare and most carry only things such as luncheon meat, bread, cheese and sausage meat. Eastern European markets also sometimes contain stocks of baby milk powders and these, combined with maize granules/flour (Polenta) etc., can produce a decent base mix for boilies. Try to bring some enhancer and a flavour to add to your mixes as this will perk up the bait, but remember to place them in well sealed containers or else your clothes will stink like an Indian restaurant!

If you intend to use fish baits for predators such as pike, zander, cats etc., you should have no problem in catching plenty of small bait-sized fish on most of the waters that you visit abroad, using basic baits such as bread, worm or corn. Saltwater deadbaits are usually easy to find but can be scarce around inland villages of Turkey and Eastern-bloc countries.

Be warned that outside the Belgium-Holland-England triangle, the countries are not geared up for bivvies and long stay anglers and you are forced to use campsites. I generally travel with a lightweight tent nowadays and this dispenses with a cumbersome umbrella.

Only a few countries, such as Sweden and Norway, allow you to wander freely with a tent (this does not mean that all the fishing is free, as many waters are private) and most other countries stipulate that you must use a campsite. There are, of course, exceptions to the rule and it is worth approaching the landowner/ private club for permission to stay overnight at the waterside. Some very wild and desolate areas allow you to camp unobtrusively, but do try to be as quiet as the beautiful nature around you and leave the area as if you've never been there. Also, be aware of the protected wildlife areas and breeding seasons.

If you intend to use boilies abroad and you are unsure of the number of nuisance fish in the water that you intend to fish, I would advise on specially preparing your baits. On some marshland waters the small roach/rudd/bream can be a very big headache and I would advise bring very large and hard boilies (I like to dry my baits out for several days). Small toothed fish, such as the American catfish can be an even bigger problem and without very large and hard baits you will be constantly rebaiting your rods.

Whilst on the subject of fishing for carp, it might be worth mentioning a common fault with many people when tackling very large and underfished lakes. A great deal of time and effort has to be put into most of these waters to deliver the goods, and if you only have a couple of days it is advisable to leave a big water well alone (unless, of course, you or your friends know the lake very well already).

An excerpt from a letter from a holiday angler will give you an idea of what I mean:

"…Well, we fished it for three solid days and never so much as saw a carp. I feel that something might have happened since you fished it, or since you got your information. It's possible the carp were in an area of the lake (Rabandages) we couldn't reach…. I admit that we don't have much experience on large (4 miles long!) lakes, but I still felt we should have caught. Have you any ideas as to why we failed?"

The lake in question actually holds a number of carp, with some reaching 40lb. I think if you read the Jens Bursell interview you will understand just how many days can go by on a 'big' water with no signs of fish, even during heavy baiting campaigns.

I will include part of a letter from another correspondent (Harry R. Million) to give you an idea of how worthwhile finding new waters can be. Even though

Harry and his companions made the mistake of only fishing Samsjon (lake) for a short period, they did find a new and exciting river nearby which held hard fighting commons. (In fact, two Danish anglers were fishing on Sam lake about the same time as Harry and after going fishless for two weeks using boilies, they suddenly started catching and landed two of the biggest carp caught that year - 1990). I will include most of Harry's letter as it contains useful information for anglers contemplating visiting the area:

Dear Tony,

I thought I would drop you a line telling you how our party of anglers got on in the wilds of Västergötland, Sweden.

Many thanks once more for your help and advice on tackling the wide and varied selection of waters that confronted us. I can see what you meant by two weeks being a very short time regarding exploring the area, but what follows could (hopefully) be useful to you.

We ventured North East straight after hitting Göteborg and settled in Skarv village to try out the string of lakes around Skara, Skarv and Lerdals as suggested. Getting onto the waters proved as difficult as seeking local advice for the area - a headache. The results were poor on these waters. Skarvalingen (the main lake) held roach, perch, tench, pike, zander and burbot but had to be fished by boats as bankside access was a near impossible task here. Tickets from Folke Gilslander at the nearby farmland, price 10 kroners (£1.00).

The nearby lake of Grönsjön - decent sized and connected to a few smaller waters by streams, contained pike, perch up to $4\frac{1}{2}$lb have been taken, roach, tench and bream, but we failed to find any carp in the area. I did suspect seeing two from up a tree with binoculars but wasted hours sitting over boilies without action, before moving on. The lake area of Grönsjön can be fished free of charge if you approach the farmer/owner with a friendly enough smile - despite the 'Fishing Forbidden' signs.

Samsjön, near Annelund contained many species, but what a size! The water was absolutely massive and yet again boilies failed here, but sweetcorn took mixed bags of fish, mainly roach and bream. Tickets 30 kroners. We found a nice little pond alongside Asunden lake and a narrow canal that, according to local advice, produced a 60 kilo bag of bream to maggot and worm baits. We caught well enough on sweetcorn - roach, bream and tench - just beyond the large bed of lilies fronting the margins. This water was again free to fish, and good fun. Asunden, although a massive sheet of water, has pike and zander among other species.

Into the second week, we found a nice friendly campsite at Salterad near Borås; the river Viskan runs directly through the campsite and is free of charge if you book into the site; other stretches are available on a 10 kroner ticket from the military base at Rydhoholm outside Borås. Pike, zander, perch, roach, bream, carp and trout, along with other species, are for the taking here. We caught a variety on sweetcorn baits tried in a variety of ways, good bags of roach, bream, a few perch and rainbow trout, along with a number of common carp, ranging from 15lb+ up to $22\frac{1}{2}$lb and a single mirror carp of $16\frac{1}{2}$lb. The carp in Viskan river took sweetcorn only; I tried getting them onto meat baits and boilies but gave up and caught on the corn baits adequately enough, being prepared to settle for mixed bags.

Näbbasjon near Borås contains pike - a funny colour, almost spotted (like newts), and zander. The lake is free of charge as with a nearby zander water and difficult to get near to for swampland surrounding the lake. Lures are popular on Näbbasjon and the Viareds area of lakes but the water is snaggy and beware of elks!!

We had enough water to keep us going - in fact that was the problem - too much. I could have stayed on for months given half a chance. I will get back to explore further. Most of the waters have not been fished at all, the only problem is location as you mentioned previously. Our stay was a rather rainy one and we were rained off most waters throughout our stay. Two weeks of solid rain, it was unbelievable, especially as our arrival back in the U.K. was a blazing sunny one!

We all enjoyed Sweden and everybody thanks you for your help in putting us onto some excellent wild waters fishing…"

To give you an example of what can be achieved if you tackle a 'BIG' water in the right way, I will give a short account of a trip I made to a very large Scandinavian water in August, 1990. I only spent one day on the water and used only one rod, but would not have attempted fishing without understanding the immense amount of groundwork already made on the lake by my Danish friends.

It was 1400 hours on the 14th August when both myself and my daughter, Amber, stepped off the train. Jens came to meet us at the station and we decided to order a taxi to drop us off within a short walking distance of the lake. Jens was glad of the welcoming luxury that the taxi provided, as his feet were covered in blisters from walking many kms in sweaty old Wellington boots that were two sizes too big! As we walked through a deep canopy of woods towards the lake, Jens brought me up to date on the fish that had been caught by himself and Danish friends recently. During July, 18 carp over 22lb had been landed with 7 over 30lb. The best were 35½lb, 37½lb and a fantastic 44lb linear mirror! The best common weighed 31lb..

The July trip had been a long one and most of the carp were caught during the first week. Jens had gone for more than 20 days without a fish and it was mainly because he had lost a carp estimated at 50lb+ after a hard fight that he had chosen to return alone for a four day trip.

Jens was now into the third day of his trip and, judging by the smile on his face, he had been catching. On the 12th, his first day, he had managed to land a wonderful 33lb/35lb brace of mirrors. The following day he landed a 28½lb linear mirror and that morning, just before coming to meet us, he had caught another 30lb+ mirror - no wonder he was smiling!

After setting up camp and having a quick tour of the area, we both decided to spend an hour stalking, as we had seen some big commons amongst the lilies in a small backwater. Shortly after we were in position, the sun sank below the high trees and the basking carp quickly departed from the cooler, shaded water, so we decided to get back to camp and set up the gear before nightfall.

Jens had decided to fish in a completely new swim for his last day. Not only was it a new swim but an entirely different lake than the one he had been fishing the last few days! I was a little upset that we were to fish the last day on an entirely unfished swim on a different lake, because I was keen to get some action, but Jens' explanation calmed me down a little. It seemed that not only was this the lake that

Jens had lost his 'fifty' from, but he had also been walking every day, over miles of rough terrain, in his wellies just to bait this very swim.

Out in front of us stretched hundreds and hundreds of acres of completely featureless water and I was more keen on trying a swim with more features, but Jens assured me that this was the kind of area where he had had earlier success with the 'biggies', so we both decided to give it a try.

I had brought no rods with me because Jens had kindly offered to loan me an old 2lb test curve carbon rod with one eye missing and a large spooled 157 cardinal. The rod had a nice, compound 'soft' feel when bent and the missing eye didn't seem to make too much difference - it was better than no rod anyway!

Jens catapulted plenty of big baits into the baited area and I made a mental note of where to cast. We cast out all the rods tight into the baited area and settled down for the night. I took the left hand side and Jens took the right hand side with his other two rods.

During the night, the water in front of us became a mirror image of my beloved 'Springpool', as carp after carp heaved their mighty weights towards the starlights and crashed with a heavy thudding sound back into the ink-like water. Hordes of kamikaze mosquitoes continually dive bombed our heads and we covered our bodies with gallons of stinking repellent to try and ward off the attack.

Jens was fast asleep aboard the luxury comfort of his bedchair, whilst both my daughter and I lay on the ground aboard soggy carry-mats that any minute threatened to sink into the oozing medieval swamplands that lay beneath us. The crashing continued through the night but not a single bleep came to the Optonics. Jens said that he had had most of his runs in the early morning, but come dawn all we got was a heavy dose of wind blown rain.

Things were getting decidedly uncomfortable for my daughter and I and we were glad when the rain gradually eased off. Shortly after the rain stopped both Jens and I noticed a couple of carp top over the baits; then, all of a sudden, Jens' right hand Optonic burst into life. There was nothing 'English-lake-butt-ringer' about this take, as the indicator very, very slowly crept towards the top of the needle. Jens was fishing with both bail arms closed and as the indicator reached the top, he lifted the rod quickly over his right shoulder. The strike was stopped halfway by a solid resistance and there was no doubting that a 'biggie' was on.

The fish made a short, 30 yard run and after only 5 minutes it was wallowing over the deeply sunk landing net which I gently lifted to engulf its huge bulk. The water exploded and once the fish calmed down, I grasped the net above the fish to take pressure off the landing net arms, and lifted. I lay the fish gently onto the long grass and unfurled the netting. WOW! What a fish! Jens slapped my back with joy and ran off with clouds of mud flying off his wellies, to fetch the weighing scales. Amber looked at the colossal 'lump' of scales lying in the net and said, "I didn't realise you were fishing for fish like that Dad, I thought you were after fish like this…" She then placed her hands apart and the gap suggested a two ounce roach!

Jens came gasping back with the scales, so I gently slipped the beautiful fish into the weigh sling. Jens tried to lift the fish on the scales but he was shaking so much that he couldn't do it! I took over; with my legs apart and a firm grip on the scales, I began to lift - 33 - 36 - 37lb - and the fish stayed firmly stuck to the floor; 38 - 39 - 40lb and Jens' eyes lit up like diamonds. I lowered my hands and slowly

*Jens with his fantastic brace – 42lb and 33lb+.*

began again - 39 - 40 - 41 - Jens started dribbling - the fish started to lift off the ground and the scales stopped at 42lb!! I lowered the fish down to the ground as Jens suddenly tried to kiss everyone (yuk!) and then dashed through the shrubs and undergrowth, screaming and jumping like a madman and punching the air as if he'd scored the winning goal in the World Cup Final.

The fish was sacked to wait for better light for the photos and calmness once again reigned supreme in this beautiful medieval vastness of forests, lakes and teeming wildlife.

Half an hour went by, when suddenly a carp topped close to Jens' right hand rod and was also travelling in that direction. Ten minutes later, the Optonic again burst into life and another very slow take developed. This fish put up a much better fight and at one stage went through a bottom snag about 60 yards out, but Jens managed to free it with constant pressure. After one exciting run along the bank, the fish was eventually brought close enough to land. The carp suddenly tried to get into the roots at our feet and I quickly placed the net in its path and it swam straight in. Not a sound came from the landing net as I held it in the deep water and turned around to look at Jens. He thought that the hook had pulled at the last moment and that it was not caught in the mesh, with the carp now long gone.

"Have you got it?" he shrieked in panicked alarm.

"No problem Jens" I calmly replied and then showed him the big common lying in the net.

Jens again lost his cool and started his native backslapping and voodoo dancing….

Jens had forgotten to bring spare carp sacks with him, so we were forced to take some pictures of this magnificent brace (33lb and 42lb) immediately. We also tried to take a few shots of my daughter with the fish, but all of a sudden she got up and started screaming! Red ants were everywhere and she was being bitten badly. We quickly returned the fish and after some problems nursing the common (we later realised why), they both strongly swam off.

We had, up to now, been using very large and hard boilies, balanced perfectly by a rock hard floater. The double boilie was lowered into the margins to check for balance and pieces were bitten off the floater until it sank very slowly. The black cotton hair was attached to the eye of the hook and the 25lb silkworm hooklengths were between 12-16 inches, with a normal running $1\frac{1}{4}$ ounce lead connected by a 5-6 inch rotten length of line so that it would break off if snagged.

We had started to experience twitches and a couple of slow takes but no strikes connected, and although some of these were, no doubt, roach, I was sure that some of them had been carp. I reasoned that the carp were moving **very** slowly along the bottom, feeding on minute foodstuffs and when they came upon a boilie they just hoovered it up while continuing to feed on the natural food. Because they were moving off with the bait so slowly, they had plenty of time to eject the bait and indeed, with some of the fish this was happening. I decided to change my rig and try and hook them before they could 'test' it. The lead paternoster was shortened to about $2\frac{1}{2}$-3 inches because I had not felt that a 2oz lead that I had cast out earlier sink too deeply into the silt. The hooklength was also shortened to about $3\frac{1}{2}$-4 inches and once the two boilies were mounted, I wrapped the hair (tied to the eye) around the shank twice, so that the bait sat tight to the bend of the hook.

Instead of balancing the baits, I chose to leave them completely buoyant. On such a short hooklength, a shot was unnecessary and the bait was anchored by a 1$^{1}/_{2}$oz lead alone. I reasoned that the carp were now at the end of their feeding period and that a pop-up would more likely be picked up by a patrolling carp, even if the fish were not prepared to 'feed' on the bottom baits.

Within minutes of recasting, the indicator slid up the needle and I struck into a giant of a fish - the roach put up a gallant fight on the heavy carp gear and must have weighed all of 2oz. Jens and Amber, amongst fits of laughter, rushed off to fetch the camera. Unfortunately, the roach was foul hooked so didn't count, and I threw it back before the photo session could commence...

I couldn't believe my luck. How could I possibly land a poxy roach after Jens had just returned a 30 and a 40? I was still convinced that a pop-up would work however, so I persevered. I tightened up very tight to the lead after casting, but realised after a single bleep that I would have to change the indication set up. Pop-ups generally attract roach like glue and because I was tight to the lead, I could easily foul hook a roach but not realise it (because it would be unable to pull out the line) and sit for hours with it attached to the hook. I decided to remain with closed bail arm (I was not actually using clips, because Jens had also forgotten his clips! Instead, I loosened the rear drag on the reel with just enough friction to aid self-hooking, but was still able to give line before everything was dragged into the drink), but this time leaving a short drop on the indicator so that I would know whether a roach was foul-hooked. The set up would still bolt any carp once it picked up the bait.

Within a few minutes of recasting, the indicator moved up, the line tightened and just as the rear drag began to give out line, I struck into a solid wall. The rod keeled over like rubber and the line went out at a fantastic rate of knots. Tightening up the drag made no difference whatsoever, and it was not before it was about 85-90 yards out that it changed direction and swam off to the left. I ran along the bank, lifting my rod over a small tree at one stage so that I could keep up with the fish. Deep swamp lay to my left and I was forced to stop before I disappeared into the ooze up to my neck. The ratchet tick-tacked as yard after yard of line continued to pull off the reel. I glanced down at the big spool and could see that the line was dangerously low. Another fast run could easily despool me. During the first run, I had felt a small 'pull' and was afraid that the hook had slipped. Was the hook embedded in a tough area of the mouth, or only held by a thin shred of skin?

I decided to risk it, and clamped down hard on the spool as Jens' eyes popped as the old rod bent like it's never bent before. It stopped! Lifting the rod high, I then wound down hard until the rod was level with the water and then lifted again. The fish felt like it was snagged but I could see the line moving slowly to the left - it must be just the weight of the fish, I thought to myself!

When the fish was about 80 yards out, it suddenly broke surface. The length of the fish was incredible. A big dorsal fin lay erect on a boat of a fish. It was then that I began to shake involuntarily and said in my mind, "please don't let me lose this fish!"

Just at that moment, my daughter spoke, "I hope you don't lose it, Dad!"

"Shutuuuuuuup!!" I screamed and the sweat started dripping off my forehead.

"*Don't lose it dad!*"

*Tony, and his daughter Amber, proudly displaying the forty pounder.*

Suddenly, I could see the lead climbing up the line as I gained more yards. I couldn't believe it; the lead had somehow become trapped on the line. I had horrible visions of it being trapped in the top eye and me having to hand-line the fish! As the dangling lead got nearer, I walked back and lowered the rod tip to let Jens untangle the lead. He reached up to grab the lead, found it to be free running and with a wry smile, swung the lead downwards and my heart stopped missing beats as I watched the lead sliding back down the line.

The fish was on the surface more often now and, although it was still putting up a fantastic fight, I was really giving it stick and it was soon close to the margins. As soon as its head came to the surface again, I was determined to keep it there and with continual pressure I walked the fish back into the waiting net held by Jens. Jens waited until the fish was almost at the spreader block, then lifted. It was then that my heart leapt for joy as I knew the fish was safe!

As soon as Jens lifted the fish, I knew it did not have the great depth of the 42 pounder, but what an incredible length! Jens said that it was the longest carp he'd ever seen on the bank and we both realised that this fish was **well** over $3^{1}/_{2}$ feet. The carp lay in the weigh sling and I lifted - 25 - 30 - 36. We both looked at the fish and it remained glued to the deck! I lowered my hands and smiled at Jens, then continued again - 37 - 38. I again lowered the scales and we both laughed at each other.

"Well, here goes, Jens", I said, 39 - $39^{1}/_{2}$ - 40lb!! Wow! **TWO** forties and a thirty in less than three hours. Fantastic!

The photo session went smoothly, only marred by me having to nurse the fish before it swam off strongly. I later realised that it was the ants! When I laid it on the carry-mat, the red ants had crawled all over the fish and began pumping it with acid. The ants also crawled all over my legs and body and caused excruciating pain (especially when one bit into my foreskin!), no wonder the poor fish was lethargic!

It was a wonderful experience to take part in the biggest trio of carp caught in one day in Scandinavian history, but what may not be realised is the hundreds of hours of blanks and many thousands of boilies that preceded this catch. Thousands of acres of lake need a **great** deal of water watch and study, so please never treat them as you would a small English lake. Jim Gibbinson's book, 'Big Water Carp' contains a great deal of good advice for anglers wishing to attempt large waters for the first time.

Big rivers are an even bigger problem, and I would advise those tackling big rivers to read carefully Leon's chapter on French rivers. Big fish in the big rivers of Europe travel over immense distances throughout the year, whether they be carp, cats, barbel or pike and I would suggest moving swims regularly to try and keep in touch with the fish. I have found that very good looking swims can sometimes be completely devoid of fish for long periods of time and sometimes I have travelled 10-20 miles up or downstream before I have connected with a group of big fish.

Wherever you decide to tackle big fish abroad, I wish you luck, and above all, enjoy yourselves - I know I do!

# Belgian Biggies

## Rini Groothuis
## translated by
## Leon Hoogendijk

Many of the years that I've been fishing for carp have been spent on the banks of a canal. I live in the south of Holland, near the Belgian border and the choice of canals is considerable. Both Holland and Belgium are rich in this type of water - long, watery channels cutting through the country in a very monotonous way. The canal attracts me; the carp are of a special kind, although there are characteristic differences between carp populations in Dutch and Belgian canals.

Many of the Dutch canals contain a large head of carp, as they are stocked with them every year by the local clubs. Some of the Dutch canals really hold an enormous carp population, like the very famous Twente Canal. Most of the carp are of the common variety (+- 90%) and many of them are between 5 and 10kg. These commons are bred in Holland and contain some 'wild blood' (25%), as they are descended from the original Dutch wildies. They are normally long, lean shaped fish, very beautiful with exceptional fighting abilities. It's no exception to catch five or more of these carp during one night from a well baited swim. Although real monsters live in some of the Dutch canals, their number is very limited and the chance of catching one is like buying a lottery ticket.

For the real 'big specimen' hunter, it's far better to put their efforts into the Belgian canals, which are the real 'mecca' of monster canal carp. I like to fish the Belgian canals because the carp are heavy and strong, with big tails and fins. There are both common and mirror carp, both varieties of a strain that converts food into body weight quickly. I am impressed by these carp; they have yet to be counted or weighed and are adding value to the mystery in which the canal is cloaked. Even to the most experienced carp anglers, who have learned to fish these canals successfully, the canal will never show them all her secrets…

Belgian canals are generally understocked waters with enormous areas of water. Some canals are frequently interrupted by sluices, and in some parts of the canal, between different sluices, you can find differences in carp populations. The canals are only occasionally stocked with carp, but when this happens it's only in a certain part of the canal between two sluices. For that reason, the average size of the carp can be different in different parts of the canal between the sluices; also their numbers will vary in each part.

However, Belgian canals contain fewer carp than Dutch canals, but what's more, many hundreds of acres have never been fished for carp before, although enormous carp are there, waiting to be caught! These fish have grown big on the natural food which the canal offers them in large quantities and therefore anglers' baits will often not be recognised as food. Although the population is small it is an ideal situation which offers the fish a chance to grow very big, up to a record size! At the same time, this situation offers the angler a unique possibility to fish for the big ones only. There's less chance of small and medium sized fish populating a baited swim, so don't expect a lot of action - there are simply not enough carp for that - but the day your monkey climber does move, there's a chance to strike into the fish of a lifetime, a true monster of unbelievable size! This has happened to my brother, Bram, who was one of the first to fish the Belgian canals seriously.

In the Autumn of 1986, he discovered an interesting length of canal, about 10 kilometres in length, between two sluices. This section has a lot of bankside vegetation, bushes and trees. A lonely carp angler wouldn't be noticed too readily, which is important, as nothing on earth attracts a carp angler more than seeing another carp angler. For this reason, bivvies etc., were not used.

That autumn was a period of pioneering in which we learned the value of particles in this type of water; swims that were baited with boilies only didn't attract any carp. To start with we didn't know exactly why this was so, but we discovered the real reason for this. In waters where the carp have never been fished for before, they don't recognise boilies as food. These monsters live all their lives in an undisturbed environment and have grown big on a balanced diet of natural food, which this environment offers them. They are not waiting for anglers' baits; they don't know what boilies are. Even if you put loads of boilies in a swim, no matter what colour or flavour, they won't recognise them as food. In my opinion, a boilie is definitely not an instant bait. Perhaps the paste of which they are made is but, after boiling, the skin around the bait will reduce the diffusion of free soluble amino-acids drastically and with this the instant reaction is lost.

In a situation with very few carp, in ratio to a big water area, there are in my mind two solutions possible. One is to prebait loads of boilies during many, many weeks, until the carp finally start taking them. The other possibility is baiting with an instant bait which will be eaten by carp immediately. For this reason, Bram was baiting with soaked maize, supplemented with strawberry boilies to give more 'body' to the baited swim.

Now, fishing a canal means dealing with boat traffic. As in most Dutch canals, the boat traffic in Belgian canals is intensive; every now and then a boat passes by and causes such a strong current that baiting a swim efficiently becomes impossible. The same problem will arise every time that a sluice is opened and so the water is moving all the time. It's not before ten o' clock in the evening that the boat traffic stops and although the current never stops completely, this is the time

*Rini Groothuis returns a Belgian canal twenty plus.*

to prebait your swim. The baited area will only be effective during the night until the boat traffic starts again early next morning.

By the way, I should tell you some interesting things about our prebaiting of the canal swim. We didn't use catapults or bait droppers for the job; particles especially, will be spread out too much before reaching the bottom when baiting a canal swim in this way because of the ever moving water. Even when using a bait dropper, the current will spread out the baits over a large area. The boilies will sink much quicker than the particles, resulting in the particles being presented many yards further than the boilies are, and so a part of the effectiveness of the prebaiting will be lost. The important thing is to prebait a certain quantity of bait in a very compact way in the spot that you intend to fish, in order to concentrate the carp's activities exactly where you are going to place your hookbaits. For this reason, the boilies were frozen into big cubes, using Tupperware boxes. These cubes were thrown into the swim by hand, and sank to the bottom where they formed a compact, concentrated presentation of free baits. Every evening six of these cubes were thrown in the swim and a small quantity of boilies were fired out tight to the baited spot.

That autumn, Bram caught four carp, the biggest being a magnificent common of $32\frac{1}{2}$lb. The capture of this fish made the start of the new season in June 1987 looked promising. After a week of prebaiting the swim started to come alive, two days before the opening date. Every now and then big fish could be seen moving slowly on the surface. They were there!!

The first day produced, after a slow, ten minute battle, the first fish of the season - a well deserved mirror of 30¾lb. Bram returned home, satisfied; not only 'the first ship was over the dam' but the situation looked promising. A second thirty was surely not impossible?

Bram never did long sessions on the canal. In the first place, night fishing was not allowed and in the second place he didn't want to attract too much attention from other anglers. For the rest of the week Bram had no more action, but even after four blank sessions his confidence was still sky high. Around midnight on the Sunday night he'd heard an incredible crash of a jumping monster carp; it seemed that an adult cow had fallen into the water! A carp of unbelievable size had thrown itself out of the water, right in the centre of the canal and had fallen back into the water, causing an enormous splash. They were still there!!

It was Monday, exactly one week after opening day; the sky was misty, the grass was wet. Pike and perch were chasing around in pursuit of small fish which broke the surface frequently, an evident sign that the fish were active: hopefully the carp were also, Bram must have thought as he cast out his baits at the start of his sixth session.

Not long after this he had a run. After a nervous battle with a fast swimming carp which made some long runs, this wild fighting fish came into the net; too wild to be heavy - a common of 24lb. Twenty minutes later another take. The monkey climber rose, fell back, and rose again until everything became tight. After he'd struck into the fish, the rod took on an enormous curve. It seemed that he'd struck into a heavy sack filled with sand, but slowly the sack started moving! The reel was 'clicking' slowly and yard after yard was taken from the spool. This was big, very big!!! Bram felt reserved power which could explode at any moment - but it never happened. The fish wasn't fast, but slow and regular, like a locomotive. There was something threatening in this battle, but no fish can ignore constant heavy pressure of a 2½lb test boron carp rod, not even this one. After about twenty minutes he came to the surface and could be netted. It turned out to be a common, but one of gigantic size. After being banked the fish was weighed and measured immediately: 39½inches long; girth 36 inches; weight 53lb 12ozs.

Because this was a record, the next day the fish was weighed again, but this time officially, and still weighed 52½lb. During the night he (I should say she - the fish was a female) had lost 1¼lb. This fish still holds the official Belgian record.

With this incredible catch, the story didn't come to an end. A record fish attracts a lot of public attention - good reason for Bram to give it a rest, but in October 1987 he did go back. I was just working on my personal computer with the manuscript for my book "Jacht op grote karper (big carp hunting), when he phoned me to ask if I could come and take some pictures. In the same swim, Bram had again caught a heavy weight, this time a mirror of 38½lb!

I would like to have joined him on his next session, but I couldn't, I had to finish the manuscript before the deadline and had only 3 weeks left. Later, I would regret this. The carp were really feeding; the baiting campaign had now really become productive. One week later I would again take some pictures of the most impressive mirror that I've ever seen in my life; a piece of dynamite, weighing 40½lb. The battle with this carp had taken over 45 minutes and Bram couldn't remember ever having caught a more powerful carp. This giant had taken over 70

Rini's brother Bram with two of his huge canal fish, $38^1/_2$lb (top) and the Belgian record of $52^1/_2$lb (below).

*Bram again with another monster mirror. This one weighed 40¹/₂lb*

yards of line from the spool several times. Halfway into the fight the fish stopped moving and lay motionless, sulking on the bottom in the centre of the canal. After five minutes of pulling in every possible direction, the fish still didn't move. Bram had given up hope and slackened his line, but one minute later the fish started moving again and took 50 yards of line from the spool. Finally, Bram won the fight, although for a long time it wasn't certain who would be 'knocked out' first!

Bram's final catches of that year came in December, a truly worthy end to a fantastic year. Two mirrors came into his net shortly after each other; both carp were thirties, weighing 31³/₄lb each!

The Belgian canals are waters with an unlimited potential for enormous carp, a potential which nobody can yet estimate. Since the capture of Bram's record carp, the canal fishing in Belgium has slowly started to develop and results started coming through the grapevine. Thirties are absolutely no exception, but even forties are being caught every year. The physical qualities of these fish are falling into the category of Mohammed Ali or Arnold Schwarzenegger - heavyweights, capable of dragging many yards of line from your spool and beginning to crack the fibres of your rod.

The fact that on some Belgian canals night fishing will now be allowed during the summer months, raises the question as to how long it will take before Bram's record is broken. Bram is sure that his fish wasn't the biggest in the canal and once saw a much bigger fish, which he doesn't dare estimate. The canals nowadays have a strong pulling power on the real big fish hunters. It's for sure that waters like the Albert canal contain record carp. Stories about carp emptying the spool of a reel are no lies. The Albert canal is probably the most horrible canal in all Belgium; very wide, a strong current, intensive boat traffic and a dangerous 'talud-of-beton' are typical characteristics of this water. You need to be a hard, experienced carp angler to stand this kind of fishing - surely not for me.

Fortunately, Belgium has smaller canals with a lot of bankside vegetation and nice peaceful surroundings, but the charm of these waters is not only physical; the real charm is the mystery which goes along with fishing them. The possibilities of hooking a fish of unknown proportions is always there. Nobody can tell you, with any authority, how big the biggest is.

If you want to catch such a heavyweight, you should know where the feeding areas are. Of course, this rule applies to every water, but this information is of vital importance on big waters like the canals. It is the key to success; a lock which is difficult to open in such a monotonous water as the canal, to find where the real hot spots are – and these are few and far between. The fish can disappear out of your 'action radius' for days, even weeks, contrary to more closed and intimate waters where, although the fish can move, this movement is always limited. The carp in such a pool or lake can't disappear; sooner or later they will be back in your swim. In canals this is different; here the fish can really disappear, perhaps moving miles from a once productive swim.

Once you've made your choice of swim you need to have confidence. Normally, hot spots can be found wherever the monotonous character of the canal can be broken by bridges, harbours, sluices, wider parts of the canal and any type of snag or holding area. In places where there is a warm water output from a factory or electricity centre a lot of action can be expected during the winter months. Carp can be caught from the centre of the canal as well as in the margins in very shallow water, but the best places are the taluds (sharp changes in the angle of the slope), which often contain large carpets of mussels - food source number one for the canal carp. Fishing on such a carpet of mussels is always a good choice.

Finally, another hint. In Belgium many fishing matches are organised every year; Belgium match anglers are some of the best in the world. They bait heavily with their secret ground baits which only contain the best quality ingredients, like bird-droppings, bloodworms and hemp, all of which are highly attractive to carp. After such a competition, when all the match anglers have gone, the carp angler arrives; he casts his baits out at a distance where the match anglers have baited up. The sun goes down, the boat traffic has stopped. Now the carp can come...

*A misty dawn with the Plön Lake system.*

*Tony Davies-Patrick returns a big common to a Scandinavian water.*

*Left: Jens Bursell with a high backed 34lb Swedis mirror.*
*Below: Johnny Jensen with a superb Swedish mirror.*

*Jens Bursell returning a huge Swedish mirror.*

*Tony Davies-Patrick proudly holds his 40lb+ Swedish mirror.*
*A big Dutch common makes a powerful surge as the sun sets on the misty canal.*

# Tour of Germany

## West Germany

Surprisingly, when an English angler thinks of a fishing holiday, he will rarely think of including Germany. In past years, it has been left to members of the British Armed Forces to taste what it has to offer.

I have spent a lot of time in Germany. As a young boy I lived, for three years, in Münster; spent seven years in the Royal Army Veterinary Corps; travel the length and breadth of the country every year and to top all this, my ten year old daughter now lives there. In spite of all this, I have spent comparatively little of that time actually fishing, and usually crossed Germany only to get to another country to fish. I am now beginning to take this large country more seriously and leave the Autobahn more often nowadays in search of its wonderful waters.

Stay with me, while I go on a 'shopping spree' through the length and breadth of Germany - I'm sure that quite a few of you will have 'bought a ticket' before you finish this chapter!

Let us begin in that lovely area in the north, known as Schleswig Holstein. Many of you will recognise the similarity of this area with Denmark - this is because it was once part of Denmark before the war and it still contains many Danish town names.

Our first 'shop' is the 'Harrods' of the German holidaymakers - the island of Sylt. You will see the shape of this island plastered on the backs of many 'upper crust' Mercedes and BMW's as they rush towards the Westerland's sandy coast and expensive restaurants. We are shopping for 'fish in the water' and not 'birds on the beach' so we turn our backs on the long legs and sand at Rantum village and cast our rods into Rantum-Becken. This is quite a large lake ($1^{1}/_{2}$km long and 2-300 metres across), which holds good carp, tench, pike, zander and eels. To the north of the lake is a stream system which runs through a series of lakes and pools along the eastern arm of the island and holds trout, carp, tench, pike, etc.

Crossing over the famous Hindenburg dam back to the mainland, we drive south on the B5 towards Bredstadt and cross both the Lecker Au (25km long) and Bongsieler (50km) canals, which both hold good fish. The best area is where the two canals join at the 37 acre Bottschlotter lake which contains good tench, 12lb+ zander, 20lb+ pike and carp over 25lb.

Driving east along the B201 towards Shleswig, we cross the Treene river at Treia. The upper reaches near Eggebeck and Tarp have some lovely overgrown banks to fish for brownies and large sea trout. The middle stretches at Hallingstedt have produced carp to 33lb, but it is clear, after visiting the area myself, that this is not the best area for carp - normally bream, asp and sea trout are caught here. A much better area for carp is the large reed flanked bend at Schwabstedt, with also the chance of occasional catfish. At Friedrichstadt, before it enters the Eider, the Treene runs into a 370 acre lake which contains double figure carp, pike and good catfish.

The Schlei fjord cuts deep into the countryside for over 40km until it reaches Shleswig - a great place for wandering in a boat. The Selker Noor arm near Selk is one of the best areas with plenty of pike, zander, eels, tench and wild carp.

The river Eider has produced some hefty fish - pike to 30lb+, carp to 37lb+ and 20lb zander. The best area lies between Breiholz and the Audorfer lake in Rendsburg.

Just west of Kiel lies the lovely Westensee Nature Park. All the lakes in the area provide good fishing for tench, carp, pike, zander and bream. These include the large 679 acre Westen lake; Brahms/Warder lake; the 105 acre Vollsledter lake and the two Schieren lakes, situated on the southern side of Westen lake. Just 15km east of Kiel, lies the 864 acre Dobersdorfer lake, containing good zander, carp and pike.

Travelling south-east on the B76, we come to the town of Plön. For a family holiday, this is probably the best place in northern Germany to base yourself, with literally hundreds of lakes of every conceivable size in a comparatively small area. Plön town lies on the northern banks of the huge Plöner Great lake. This 7,507 acre (!) lake with depths up to 60 metres is connected to a vast network of lake systems joined together by small streams. The water holds pike over 20lb, 15lb+ trout, good tench and bream to 14lb+. On the north western edge of town lies the Plöner Lesser lake (some hefty carp in this water!) and Trammer lake; on the eastern side lies Schöh lake. Spreading out like a spider's web, is every type of water you could wish for, from big, windswept inland 'seas' to small and quiet lily strewn ponds - a paradise for someone on holiday. Quite a few of the smaller lakes contain carp to 30lb+; just ask the local anglers which ones - not enough space here. Besides, I fish some of them myself and I'd like them to stay quiet for just a little longer!

One good water worth mentioning lies 20km from Plön on the B76 at Raidorf (SW of Dobersdorf lake). Here, the river running out of Lanker lake is held up by a watermill and dam to form the Rosen lake. This 106 acre lake holds 5lb+ eels, 20lb+ pike, good catfish (up to 70lb but very few), and carp to 30lb+. Boats can be hired at the clubhouse.

As we travel south through Hamburg and Bremen, we come to Cloppenburg. 11km north of town is the wonderful Thülsfelder lake at Petersfeld. This 370 acre lake, with depths to 18ft, holds good zander, carp, pike and tench, but it is the big catfish that interest us most, with one caught in 1989 topping 108lb!

About 55km north of Thülsfelder on the B72 is the town of Leer (close to the Dutch border). Here the oxbow arm of the river Leda and the 120 acre Bagger lake produce catfish to 25lb, zander to 15lb, 20lb+ pike, 30lb+ carp and eels up to 7lb!

*Above: "It was this big mister!" The River Treene at Schwabstedt*
*Below: The upper reaches of the River Treene.*

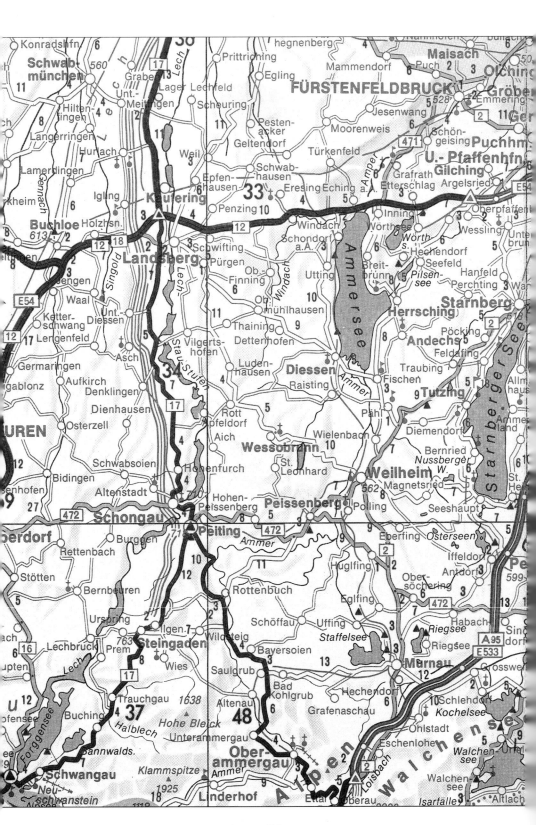

Speicher Lake, the Lech River and
Lake system, Starnberger Lake etc.,
in West Germany.

Travelling south of Cloppenburg on the B69/B51 via Diepholz, we come to the massive 1,300 acre Dummer lake at Lembruch. This is no 'dum' water either! It might be a big expanse of water, but the fish that swim in it are also big - catfish to 20lb+, carp 40lb+, eels 7lb+, pike to 46lb and zander to an incredible $35\frac{1}{4}$lb! It makes you sick, just reading about it, dunnit?

Let's get back down to earth and look for a water a bit closer to England's size and standards. Keeping on the same road, we drive to Osnabrück and then east towards the famous canal at Hengelo. 30km before the Dutch border and just 8km west of the town of Rheine, lies the Haddorfer lake, near the village of Ohne. This $29\frac{1}{2}$ acre lake is one of a six lake complex, producing pike to 20lb, tench to 7lb, double figure zander, carp to 20lb+ and some perch over 6lb. (Oh well, almost English standards!)

As we are now very close to the E30 motorway, which is the route to Berlin, I will name a couple of good waters in what was the Western Sector. (One good lake on the way, just off the E30 at Rinteln, is the Doktor lake, which lies closer to the Weser river and holds pike, eels to 5lb, 20lb+ zander and carp to 40lb+). Both the 18km long, 1,346 acre Tegeler lake and the 2,803 acre Wann/Havel lake system in Berlin hold good carp, cats, pike, zander, tench, roach, perch and very large asp. Now that the terrible Berlin wall has bitten the dust, you can nip across to the eastern sector and fish the lovely Seddin lake and be the first in your home town to have fished in east Berlin! In all honesty, if you are thinking of heading for East Germany (DDR) to fish, I would advise you to head for the northern lakeland area around Waren and Neustrelitz, an area that I hope to try during 1990-91. (See notes at the end of this chapter for more info on East Germany).

Back in the west again, we travel south from Rheine via Münster, until we cross the river Lippe at Hamm. This river holds good barbel with some reaching double figures. If we travel east from Hamm towards East Germany, we come to Goslar. Directly south of Goslar is the Harz Nature Park, which straddles the DDR border. The area surrounding Clausthal Zellerfeld holds more than 40 pools and medium sized lakes and is a good area to centre yourself. Larger lakes inside the park include Oder lake - situated at Bad Lanterberg, a 335 acre, 5km long water containing good carp (20lb+), tench, pike 30lb+, eels and trout, and the Söse lake at Osterode, which has produced 20lb+ carp and 35lb pike. The Vienenburger lake is a good water which lies NE of Goslar at Vienenburg. This 86 acre lake holds 20lb+ carp and very big pike - one fish has been recorded at almost 53lb! Another special water lies just 8km north of Vienenburg near Schladen. The Steinfelder lake is about 120 acres and holds colossal sized fish - eels to 6lb, pike to 44lb and carp to 66lb; how does that place grab you?!

This is getting a bit ridiculous, so let's drive down to good old Kassel and see what we can find. The river Fulda between Kassel and the river Werra junction at Hann-Münden produces sizeable carp and tench; pike to 20lb and catfish to 47lb+. Good barbel and chub fishing is to be had many miles upstream at Schlitz (north of Fulda). South west of Kassel at Waldeck lies the huge 1,200 acre, 27km long Ederlake. The lake was formed by damming the river Eder and holds double figure zander, some going to 28lb+, 20lb+ carp, brown trout over 10lb, tench 6lb, eels to 8lb and pike to 48lb! The area is also noted for its barbel to 7lb and large chub to $7\frac{1}{2}$lb. I only wish I could find a 2 acre lake with the same fish! The lower lake (Waller) at Affoldern holds cats over 35lb, pike and

*Above: Rosen Lake: boats can be hired at this water.*
*Below: Very big chub can be caught from the Kehnader Lake.*

zander to 20lb+ and carp to 25lb.

Travelling west on the B21 to Brilon and then west again on the B516, we come to Möhnesee. The Möhne lake (1,037 acres) with its two arms of 10 and 5km, was formed by damming the Möhne river (north of Arnsberg) and forms part of the Arnsberger Nature Park. It is yet another good chub water with some specimens reaching 6½lb. Other species include perch to 4¼lb, eels to 5lb, tench to 7lb, pike 20lb+ and many double figure zander. Further downstream, the Möhne enters the River Rühr and big chub (some reaching 10lb+!) can be caught where the river is dammed to form the Henstey, Harkorn, Kemnader and Baldeney lakes, as it winds through the Dortmund/Essen conurbation. The best of these is the Kemnader lake where an 8¼lb chub was caught in 1989. The Ruhr also contains good barbel, with some reaching double figures, especially on the stretches of gravel runs at Geisecke near Schwerte.

South of Arnsberg on the B229 is the 815 acre Sorpe lake, situated in the Homert Nature Park. This water is renowned for its rainbows and brownies, but it also holds some good carp, pike, zander and bream.

Driving south again on the B229/236, we come to Atterdorn. Here lies the 1,729 acre Bigge lake and the smaller (395 acre) Lister lake, which hold good chub and bream, carp and trout to upper doubles, perch to 5lb+, pike to 25lb, zander 12lb+ and big eels to 7½lb.

The E40 now takes us to Koln. West of Koln on the E40 near Düren, lies the Lucherberger lake which turned up a cracking 47½lb pike in 1990! Just south of Koln is the town of Bruhl. There are a group of lakes to the west of the town, offering good fishing for pike, eels, zander, tench, trout and big carp. There are a number of smaller pools, but the larger ones give a better chance of big fish. These include, Mittel lake (46 acres), Bleibteu lake (138 acres), Heider Berg lake (86 acres) and the 57 acre Berggeist lake where a carp of just under 50lb was landed in 1989, on sweetcorn.

The B265 road takes us southwest towards the lower half of the Nordtel Nature Park, between Heimback and Simmerath. Here the dammed Urft river has produced a huge lake in three arms - the Rurst/Orft lake. Big waters generally mean big fish, and this is no exception. It holds eels to 6lb+, tench, carp, double figure zander, and pike to 40lb. A wonderful 4½lb perch was landed in the Rur arm of the lake in 1990.

The large river Main holds many big carp along its length; the best in 1989 was caught near Würzberg and weighed 47½lb. The old lady Rhein herself holds monster carp. These are best sought out in the many ox-bow lakes and back-arms of the river. One of the best areas is at Karlsruhe. Many good lakes lie along this stretch of river. The best carp landed in this area during 1989 was a 51½ pounder, caught on boilie, in one of the back-arms near Neupotz.

We now head towards Switzerland, to sample some wonderful waters in the south of Germany. Nestled in the beautiful Schwarzwald, just 33 km to the north of Waldshut on the Swiss border, lies the Schluch lake. Zander over 25lb and pike to over 35lb swim in its 1,284 acres of water. East of here is the incredible 133,133 acre Boden lake (Bodensee), one of the biggest in western Europe. It holds trout over 35lb, with pike and carp to over 35lb, among a host of other species. The Uberlinger arm is one of the best areas and there are a lot of good smaller lakes close to Überlingen. Big barbel (10lb+) have also turned up at Konstanz.

*The author with a brace of roach weighing in at $2^1/_2$ and $2^3/_4$lb – from the prolific Plön system.*

The Lech river is a series of pools and lakes once it crosses the Austrian/ German border at Füssen, and on the banks of the Forggen lake is a good place to base yourself. Danube salmon, carp, catfish, trout, tench, barbel and very large pike can be caught along its length as the river leaves Forggen and drops through a series of large lakes until it reaches Konigsbrunn dam 100 km downstream. One of the best places for barbel (7-10lb), is at Denklingen. Hofen (543 acres), Bannwald (555 acres), and a number of smaller lakes to the north of Forggen, such as the 20 acre Kaltenbrunner lake at Prem, all hold good pike, perch, trout, tench and carp.

North of Boden lake and 12km south of Pfullendorf, lies the 178 acre Illmen lake which holds big pike (upper thirties), large carp and big eels, and is noted for its very big asp (15lb). The even larger Starnberg lake at 14,079 acres(!) lies to the east of Ammer and has turned up 35lb pike, 20lb+ zander, 35lb+ carp and catfish over 50lb. It is also noted for its chub reaching into double figures! Two lakes lie either side of Murnau, just off the E55 motorway. Staffel lake (1,890 acres) holds 20lb+ zander, 30lb+ pike and big carp, but the smaller 432 acre Rieg lake is, in my view, a much better option, with both pike and carp topping 40lb, eels over 8lb, 7lb tench and large bream shoals. To the south west of Rieg lake are both the Kolchel and large Walch lakes, both holding large cats, carp and pike, with Walch also holding some incredible sized chub - to match Starnberb!

A large number of smaller lakes lie closer to the river Donau near Ingolstadt. Two good, kidney shaped (173 acres) waters at Weichering (8km south west of Ingolstadt) hold 20lb+ pike, 30lb+ carp and catfish over 45lb.

*Regensburg district is reputedly the best area in West Germany for big cats.*
*Below: Thomas Vedel with a Zander of 18$^{1}/_{4}$lb*

North east of München at Ismaning, is the big 1,531½ acre Speicher lake, which runs off the Mittlerer Issar canal. It contains big carp, tench, zander, pike and eels, but is noted mainly for its huge bream over 15lb. The best landed in 1989 was a fantastic 20lb bream in wonderful condition, although sadly, the fish was killed and taken home.

The 6½km long, 2km wide, 2,198 acre Tegern lake is situated 32km south of München on the B318 and holds tench, eels, 20lb+ carp and 30lb+ pike. Directly east of Tegern is the 2km long, 543 acre Schier lake at Hausam. This water holds very large trout to 20lb, and carp over 30lb.

Let's now move north east of München into the 'big cats' area surrounding Regensberg. The 39½ acre Thenner lake that runs off the Issar river at Moosberg (south west of Landshut) holds good carp, tench and catfish (to over 90lb). The Stau lake at Hals (north of Passau), is a 5km long lake, formed by damming the Ilz river (a tributary of the Donau) and is noted for its large carp to over 40lb. Upstream from Passau on the Donau, between Vilshafen and Hofkirchen, swim barbel of over 12lb (the best at 20lb+ in 1971), very big asp to over 16lb and good chub, catfish and zander.

The Regen river is also a good barbel river, especially around Kötzting. The Blaibacher lake (172 acres) is part of the river above Blaibach and holds good carp, tench, pike, barbel and chub. The best area for catfish on the river is at Interaubenbach, near Cham, with some specimens over 79lb, and Nittenau, with fish to 125lb+. The 44 acre Wald lake near Roding has produced cats to 108lb and big pike. Just 9km north west of Roding is the 24 acre Mülweiher, holding grass carp over 20lb.

The river Naab above Schwandorf has produced big barbel in past years, but these have been more scarce recently (due to pollution?). The 111 acre backwater, close to Zeil at Main (north west of Bamburg) holds various types of large grass carp to over 35lb, zander over 20lb, pike to 35lb and mirror carp into upper thirties.

*A big mirror carp from an enclosed swim.*

# East Germany

It might be worth mentioning here, some big fish waters in the DDR, for those of you who are contemplating fishing there now that the wall has finally been taken down. I was contemplating doing complete chapters on the east communist countries, but this would have made the book just too big! A list of some big fish caught will give you an idea of what East Germany has to offer.

Carp: 52$\frac{1}{4}$lb - from the Oder-Spree canal which stretches from the river Spree and passes the towns of Müllrose and Eisenhüttenstadf before joining the mighty Oder river near Fürstenberg.
Carp: 50$\frac{1}{2}$lb - from the Templiner lake near Templin (take the 109 route north of Berlin).
Carp: 47$\frac{1}{4}$lb - from the Tonloch lake near Gollitz.

Catfish: 170lb and 148$\frac{1}{2}$lb - from the Warnow river near Oberwarnow.
Catfish: 147$\frac{3}{4}$lb - from the Fehrbelliner waterway.

Pike: almost 53lb! - from the large Brembach lake (Gobbrebach-Speicherstau).
Pike: 48$\frac{3}{4}$lb - from Tagebau-Jugendteich (Jugend lake) at Lucken.
Pike: 47$\frac{1}{2}$lb - from Hohenwarte lake.

Eel: 8$\frac{1}{2}$lb - from Weida lake (Weida-Talspere near Zeulan-Roda).
Eel: 8$\frac{1}{2}$lb - from Schwan lake near Liebrerose (north of Cottbus).
Eel: 8$\frac{1}{4}$lb - from Lang lake near Cottbus.

Chub: 11$\frac{1}{2}$lb+! - from the river Spree running into the Müggel lake in East Berlin.
Chub: 11lb! - from the Alte Elbe river near Plötzky.
Chub: almost 11lb - from the river Elde river near Kronskamp (this river runs out of the large Plauer lake at Plau).

Bream: 13$\frac{1}{2}$lb - from the Kleiner (smaller) Komber lake.
Bream: 12$\frac{1}{2}$lb+ - from the Warnow river near Unterwarnow.
Bream: 11$\frac{3}{4}$lb - from Poritzer lake.

Tench: 9$\frac{3}{4}$lb - from the Alt Elbe river near Breitenhagen.
Tench: 8$\frac{1}{2}$lb - from the Silo canal.
Tench: 8lb+ - from Staubecken at Radeburg, north of Dresden.

Perch: 6$\frac{1}{2}$lb+ - from the Mooschach lake near Eichend.
Perch: 6$\frac{1}{4}$lb - from Lübb lake near Templin.
Perch: 6lb - from Schamm lake.
Zander: 27$\frac{1}{2}$lb+! - from the Hohenwarte-talspherre (lake).
Zander: 26$\frac{3}{4}$lb - from Hohenfelden lake.
Zander: 24$\frac{1}{2}$lb+ - from the Havel.

Asp: 22¾lb! - from the river Spree near Köpenick.
Asp: 17¼lb - from the Elbe-Emflut canal.

Brown Trout: 12¾lb - from the Kiesschacht near Heringen.

Rainbow Trout: 12lb from the Lichtenberg lake.

*Although East Germany no longer exists, we haven't altered the text because the country will still be shown on many maps.

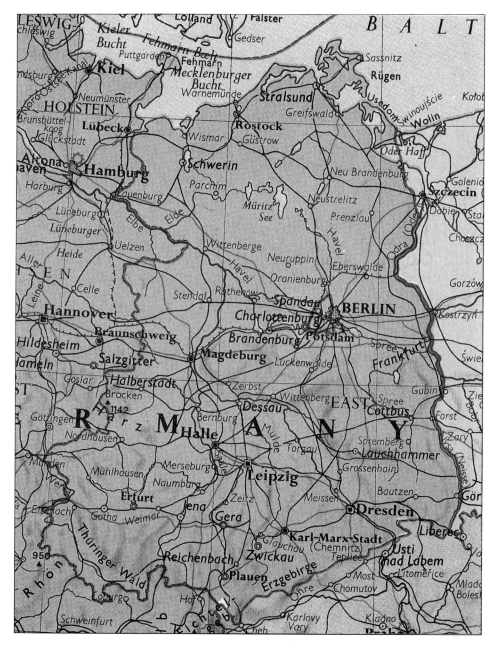

# Carp Fishing in Holland

Holland, land of mills, tulips and…carp!

Although one of the smallest countries in Europe, Holland has a lot to offer to carp anglers. When looking at a detailed map you will discover many rivers, canals, big lakes and thousands of smaller pools, many of them being excellent carp waters.

The carp don't grow as big as their French brothers and sisters, but many fish between 40 and 50lb are reported, while hundreds of thirties are caught every year, from all kinds of waters.

In the early seventies there were few carp anglers in Holland and about 90% of the waters containing carp were unfished.

*Leon Hoogendijk cradling a hard fighting Dutch common.*

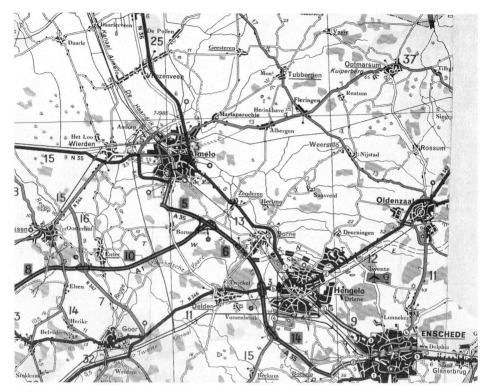

*The Twente Canal – Holland.*

In the mid and late seventies carp fishing became more popular, partly due to the articles in the angling press written by Rini Groothuis. Rini, a founder member of the Dutch Carp Study Group, was regarded as a real specialist and his catches were indeed remarkable at the time. With his articles and his book 'Karper', which was considered the bible for carp anglers, he inspired many of us (including me).

In the early and mid eighties, carp fishing 'exploded' due to the boilie and selfhooking rigs which came over from England. Carp fishing had become easier and everybody could catch some carp now without putting in a lot of time.

At the same time, something else changed; the big lakes (200 acres) which held few, but very big carp, became fishable. These big, undertstocked lakes also held large bream populations which had previously made fishing for carp with classic methods and baits unsuccessful. Because of the low density of carp, a baiting campaign over a long period was essential to transform a swim into a sort of holding/feeding area for some carp, but when baiting up with paste baits, potatoes or particles, many bream immediately took over the swim and made fishing impossible — and the baiting campaign ineffective. Now the boilie had come our way and proved to be the ultimate bait for these types of water. The big lakes had never been fished seriously before, so the carp had been growing all those years, not living under stress, and had become very big.

The big lakes of the west of Holland are probably the best, but also the most difficult, waters for really big carp nowadays. Some of the most fanatical Dutch carp anglers are putting in over 2,000 fishing hours a year on these lakes and are catching few, but very big, carp. Most of these waters hold only very small populations of mirror and leather carp but every year they produce many thirties and forties.

In the late seventies and early eighties, carp fishing in canals became popular again, partly due to the articles of Rini Groothuis but also because of the repeated reports of big carp by some individuals who fished the now legendary Twente canal in the east of Holland. Most of the Dutch canals are packed with good sized common carp and the locals on these waters are catching loads of twenties every year but some of the best canals, like the famous Twente canal, are also producing a lot of thirties and forties. Many people are fishing the Twente canal in Hengelo, in the warmer water near the salt factory or just on the other side of the sluice. The part from Hengelo to Entschede has also become popular, but near Delden and even further to the west, near Goor, you can still find excellent,

*Jack de Bliek with a common carp of 38¹/₄lb from the Twente Canal.*

48

*Famous Dutch Carp angler Leo Westdorp with a Dutch canal caught carp of 29lb.*

less pressured, swims which are packed with big carp. In some periods of the year fishing a canal can be frustrating; the carp are not feeding and the canal looks dead, but in good periods you can have tremendous catches which are not possible in other types of water. What about 57 carp, including many doubles, some twenties, and a thirty in just one weekend, or 14 twenties in 24 hours, or 4 thirties in a day! These are all catches realised in Dutch canals.

Another phenomenon in canals is the way they produce. Once a swim produces a small carp, you'll often continue catching small ones, but if you catch a big 'un you'll have a good chance of catching a few more 'biggies'. Often the canal will be dead for some days then suddenly, for no apparent reason, the fish will start feeding like mad and the fishing will be good in the whole canal. Sometimes your swim will only produce small carp, while someone who's fishing next to you doesn't stop catching big ones, so as you can see, fishing a canal is special; some people love it, some people hate it. Decide for yourself.

Another famous Dutch water of a different type is lake Sloterplas in Amsterdam (300 acres +), which is heavily stocked with mirror carp, probably the strongest concentration of carp in Holland. Catches of 36 fish a night and over 100 fish in a weekend, including many twenties and some thirties, have been reported. On one of my trips there I talked to some locals, who estimated the population at over 20,000 carp, which is quite possible.

For those of you who prefer fishing in a beautiful water in peaceful surroundings, away from the crowd, the Binnenmaas at Maasdam, near Rotterdam (south), is an excellent choice. It's an old, big dammed water containing many double figure commons up to about 25lb, and 10 carp a night is quite normal. It's a typical night water and produces best at very close range. I have used this water on occasions for testing hooks, rigs, baits etc., and more than once had two runs at the same time! It surprises me that so few people fish the water because you can really have great sport with the many good, hard fighting commons here.

Voornse-kanaal, a nice canal about 10km in length, very rich in natural food (fresh water mussels). Narrower than the Twente, between Hellevoetsluis and Heenvliet/Zwartewaal (south-west of Rotterdam) and containing a large number of big commons (20-35lb and still growing!).

In the same region there are a number of other nice waters containing big carp and pike but they are too small to mention so it's up to the readers to discover them.

The beautiful river Rotte between Rotterdam and Moerkapelle. The river is shallow with a rich mud bottom, nicely decorated with roots and lilies. From 50 to 150 yards wide and about 18km in length. Carp of any size, including very big ones, over the whole of the length.

The most interesting part is near Zevenhuizen where the river transforms into a big lake of 2km in length and from 500 to 1,000 yards wide.

The last part of the river (Moerkapelle) is also superb, very peaceful with a number of windmills and roots everywhere. No angling pressure!

It's impossible for me to sum up all the good Dutch waters I know here, there simply isn't enough space, but if you come to Holland the owner of any local tackle shop will be able to put you in the right direction.

As you can see, Holland has a lot to offer and is a real paradise for carp anglers.


NOTE.

To fish any Dutch water you'll need two permits, one national and one from the owner of the water. The national permit can be bought in a post office and the other permit can be bought in a local tackle shop.

# Kralinge Plas
# – Holland

This chapter is about the now famous (and feared) Kralingse Plas, a 300 acre lake in Rotterdam (west of Holland) and some of my experiences on this water.

The lake is old, relatively shallow, heavily overstocked with bream and understocked with carp (as with most of the bigger lakes in the west of Holland). The shape of the lake is square. During summer the place is crowded with boats, surfers and swimmers; there's a beach and a yacht harbour on the west side; the south bank consists of some bays and islands while the north and east banks are monotonous, only featured by some reeds here and there. In the south east corner there is a large bay which is connected to two smaller, shallow lakes by a narrow and shallow canal (5 yards wide and 2 feet deep).

Every spring some carp, not many, will pass through this canal and inhabit the small lakes for one or two months before swimming back to the big lake after spawning. In the past, I've also seen carp spawning between the rocks at the east and north side of the lake, but always in small groups (5 or 6 fish). There is almost no propagation because of the absence of weed beds (protection), and the enormous eel population. This absence of weed beds, combined with the same depth (8-10ft) everywhere, results in the lake not having any holding or feeding areas; the natural food and the carp are spread out over the whole lake.

In the past the carp population was over estimated but we now know that the lake only holds about 500 carp. Between 60 and 100 of these carp are big, old mirrors and leathers (20-40lb), while the rest are common carp of a later stock (5-25lb).

500 carp spread out over 300 acres of water means 5 carp every 3 acres! I hope that you get the picture now - certainly not a water to fish during your short term holidays, but a water to fish for at least one whole season! Read on…

In 1983, I took the decision to fish the lake seriously. There was no pressure at all; in fact, nine times out of ten I would be the only carp angler on the lake. An older carp angler I knew had fished the lake and caught some mid-twenties during the seventies, so I thought that the lake should hold some thirties by now. My plan was to do a lot of observation during the closed season (15th March - 27th May) and to do a lot of short sessions, moving with the wind. I started my observation sessions around mid-April, going to the lake every evening and staying just until dark.

By the end of May I had seen carp in the big lake on six occasions and in six different swims! In May I also discovered about 30 carp in one of the smaller lakes. They had formed a group and could be found in the same shallow corner every evening. I started feeding them with breadcrusts and it took 3 or 4 days before they started taking them. It was difficult to estimate their size because the water in this muddy corner was dark brown coloured and the only thing that could be seen were the tails breaking the surface, or a pair of big lips when they took the breadcrust.

May 28th, opening day. I fished a swim on the east bank. The temperature had dropped and my confidence was nil! The bait was potatoes, fished at close range, and although I had plenty of action, catching big bream every 10 minutes or so, I didn't see any sign of carp.

May 30th, I did a session on what we used to call the 'keienkant' (rockbank) because of the many rocks covering the bottom in the margins, a swim in the north eastern corner which looked promising with a south west wind blowing. However, the result was again plenty of bream but no carp!

Late in the afternoon, the wind dropped and I decided to visit the smaller lake to see if the carp that I had seen there before were still there. Well, they were still there but nothing like the number I had seen before, perhaps only 4 or 5 fish. I baited the swim with breadcrusts and they were all taken within minutes. However, when I presented my hookbait in front of their noses, they decided that they'd had enough of it and slowly moved out of the corner, one by one. I could have pulled my hair out; if only I had presented my hookbaits first...!

I sat down on the grass and smoked a cigarette, when suddenly I saw the already brown water turn black! One carp had returned to the corner and was heavily feeding on the bottom, so I cast out a small piece of potato just behind the cloud and then pulled it back slowly. I opened the bail arm and a few minutes later had a very slow take. I struck into a powerful carp and fifteen minutes later it was on the bank; my first of the season and my first from the complex, a nicely scaled mirror of 28 pounds. (Three years later, someone else caught this fish again, in the big lake, at 30lb+). After returning the fish, I checked the depth where I hooked it - only one foot deep! After this day I didn't see any more carp in the small lake for the rest of the season; they had obviously spawned and returned to the big lake.

June 2nd. I did a morning session in rainy conditions on the rockbank and saw some very big carp rolling on the surface at only 15 yards out. They were really rolling over my baits but I never had a take (no bream this time either!). Later in the morning I was disturbed by some surfers, so I stopped fishing but was back in the evening.

The rain had stopped and the gentle south west wind of the morning had gained in force. I was very confident and knew I was going to have one this evening. Ten minutes after casting, the first fish was on the bank, a bream of 65cms! One minute later I had another bream on the other rod. The strong south west wind had obviously driven a large shoal of bream into the swim and although I was fishing potatoes the size of a chicken egg, it took only a few minutes for the bream to break them into small pieces and hook themselves. The situation made me nervous; I knew the carp were still there but all I was catching were these ugly bream every 5 or 10 minutes.

I became desperate and finally put a potato as big as an orange on both rods, which I threw out by hand. This really did the trick, because after 20 minutes without a bleep I was surprised by a fast take and struck into something big. Forty yards of line were pulled from the spool before it became snagged and the hook finally came out. Shit! No time to rebait the rod because now the other one was away. I hooked a strong fish again which, during the next 20 minutes tried to bury itself between the rocks in the margins. During the whole of the fight I pulled as hard as I dared with my 2lb TC glass rod and she simply didn't manage to get between the bottom rocks. I finally landed her, a 28lb linear mirror, with an enormous mouth!

The following day I was back, but the wind had turned 180° and the carp had gone. The next eight sessions I kept moving swims but only had one small mirror from the east bank (plus about 50 big bream!). I tried black rye bread as bait, but this was not bream proof either.

June 19th. I fished a morning session in the narrow end of the yacht harbour near the sluice. The harbour was bell-mouthed, like a funnel, and with an easterly wind blowing right into it I expected that some carp would eventually be driven into this narrow end. I only used one rod with a float and cast a small piece of potato into a shallow area (3ft) near a wooden landing stage. Between six and nine that morning I had an incredible eight takes, but unfortunately managed to land only three carp, the best being an upper double mirror. At nine o' clock the sluice opened and the boat traffic made further fishing impossible. The harbour proved to be the only swim in the lake which didn't produce loads of bream; they obviously didn't like the shallow water. However, to learn more about the lake I felt that I had to move again. Eleven blank sessions followed (only bream).

July 22nd. I had a twenty from the harbour, then another thirteen blanks! (more bream).

August 15th. A shoal of about 10,000 bream inhabited my swim but weren't feeding (miracle!) and I managed to catch a good twenty from the rockbank.

The rest of the season I had countless blanks, tons of bream and a number of small commons from the harbour; I also lost one big mirror at the net. At the end of the year my conclusion was that the enormous bream population made baiting swims and fishing impossible. I decided not to return to the lake before I had solved this problem.

The answer came the following year, when the 'boilie bomb' exploded in Holland. The next three years saw me experimenting with boilies and rigs (with some friends - we emptied some lakes!) and studying the H.N.V. and L.N.V. theories. Speaking about H.N.V.'s, it soon became clear to me that an H.N.V. was a better bait; better for the health of the carp, yes, but certainly not more effective, and often less effective, than a good attractor crap bait! Discussion closed! Let's concentrate on the carp instead of the bait!!

In 1987, my mate Erwin and I decided to fish the big lake again and we fished from early May until October. What happened was described in detail in Carp Fisher No. 16 (magazine of the Carp Society), but for those who didn't read it, I will give a short account.

During six months, we literally filled in our swims with bait (mixed particles + boilies) and this resulted in the creation of an artificial holding and feeding area. We were doing our average 50 hour session every week, except for two breaks to fish a French water. All of these sessions produced numbers of fish, including many twenties and a number of thirties, which made us the most successful carp

*Kralinge Plas – The Island Pitch.*
*Below: Leon Hoogendijk's first thirty from the water in 1987.*

*Leon's terrific brace of mirrors of 34lb 13oz and 33lb 11oz*

anglers on the water. The highlight of this six month period was reached on the morning of May 21st., when Erwin caught fish of 23.12, and 28.11, while I was rewarded with fish of 33.11 and 34.13. These four fish were all caught within 3 hours! A total of about 15 carp anglers fished the lake that year and most of them were struggling. Two other carp anglers were successful too; one was fishing a swim on the east bank, with fishmeal boilies, I believe, while the other man had found another successful method. He often walked around the lake to observe, not the carp but the carp anglers, especially those who were prebaiting their swims. He then simply moved into their baited swims after they had left. During our first short trip to France it was our turn to be victims and the man caught some big carp from our swims (including a thirty!).

However, 1987 was my last, and best, Dutch carp season. I had been working hard for my catches and was completely satisfied about the obtained results. I moved to France at the end of the year.

*Leon with a very old Dutch mirror carp from a big lake. There are understocked lakes in Holland containing fifties that haven't been fished yet.*

The labels within the map:

STAKES

BEACH

LANDING STAGE

ISLAND

LANDING STAGE

ROCKBANK

ISLAND

SLUICE

HARBOUR

HARBOUR

1200 YARDS

1200 YARDS

N

Average depths between 8 and 10 feet.

MILLS

A

B

ISLANDS

KRALINGSE - PLAS

SMALL LAKES

● = Swims which produced numbers of carp.

◉ = Most productive swims

A = The shallow corner where I caught my first fish of the complex.

B = The swim where Erwin and I had our fantastic 1987 season by filling-in the swim with large quantities of bait during six months.

Why include a chapter about such a difficult water where most are struggling the whole season, you might ask. Well, when writing for the book, my intention was not only to put you in the right direction, to write about suitable holiday waters and successful methods on these waters, but also to show you the other side of big carp fishing in different countries. You will understand that the Kralingse Plas is certainly not a water which is worth spending a holiday on, as the chances that you will blank are 99.9%! Some very well known and respected Dutch carp anglers fished the water in the past, they struggled and gave up fishing the water!

Of course, the Kralinge Plas is not the only water of this type in Holland. In the west and centre, there are many of these understocked lakes, some of which are much bigger and hold bigger carp (fifties!), but have yet to be fished for carp!

*Jens Bursell with a fantastic 40$^1/_2$lb Swedish common.*

# Denmark & Sweden

## Jens Bursell talks to Tony

*Jens, when did you first become interested in fishing? Can you remember that far back…?*

Ha, ha - I'm not so old! I think the first time that I started fishing was when I was almost 10 years old. I had a little spinning rod and went down to Fure lake and I saw a big bream - at **least** a pound - on the surface, and I was very keen to catch it - and I did! Maybe it wasn't the bream I saw…

It's a lake really packed with bream and no matter how hard you try not to catch them, you will catch one! But then, my rod was stolen a few weeks later and I forgot all about fishing after that, until 2 years later when a friend took me down to Fure lake again and I started fishing.

I joined the local club because I wanted to know more about fishing, and that was the real start of my true interest in the sport. That was the winter of 1979/80. It was mostly coarse fishing and I did a lot of piking and cod fishing etc., etc.

*So you became quite a 'general' angler about this time? Can you remember your first introduction to carp fishing?*

I had for a long time been dreaming about catching either a tench or a carp and then, in 1981, I was fishing for pike when I saw a tench lying under a lily leaf. I just had to catch it. I had some worms with me so I took off the lure and replaced it with a single hook. I flicked the worm under the lily and it took it straight away! It was my biggest freshwater fish ever - a 2 kilo tench and I was very happy.

I went down again that evening and baited up with a load of sweetcorn, which I had read, in a Danish book ('Modern Medefiskeri' by Ploug Hansen), was good for tench; I knew a little about baiting up with loose feed for roach and bream. This time I baited up with rasp (breadcrumb) groundbait and baited every night and caught a hell of a lot of tench. Many of them were only 2-3lb, so in fact I was quite lucky that I caught such a large tench for my first fish.

I think I fished a lot for tench for 2 years, and then in 1982, with some of the other guys in what is now the Dansk Karusse Konsortium (D.K.K.), I started to fish another lake for tench. We caught a lot of tench up to 5lb, with an average of about 4½lb. That really got me going. We met some others at the lake whom we talked to and started night fishing with, and that became the unofficial start of the D.K.K. I also started match fishing at this time - fishing with poles, etc.

*And what was your first introduction to carp?*

Oh yes, sorry! That was when we talked with some of the guys at that lake where we had fished for tench previously, and they had caught a lot of carp up to about 10lb - mirrors…

*With the guys in the D.K.K?*

Yes, but it didn't have that name at the time. I started to fish with Jesper at first (Jesper Peterson), and then I met Claus Kvist, Ulrik Neilson and Thomas Vedel at that lake. The year after, in 1983, Jesper and I went to Lammefjord canal.

*Did you catch one on your first trip?*

Yes, we caught 25 carp. Small carp, between 1lb and 7lb. Wildies.

*That was some introduction to carp fishing!*

Yes, it was quite a good start.

*A 7lb wildie, in my opinion, is a very good fish…*

Well, 7lb is a little exaggerated, it was 2.7kg, and that's nearer 6lb.

*What was your first feeling of one of these different species?*

It was fantastic to hook a carp using quite light gear. I was using match rods and 0.20mm line. The water was packed with weeds so it was thin line for these conditions, and we were using floats with sweetcorn or bread for bait.

We went a couple of times that summer; Jesper also caught a lot of fish and we became very keen. The next year, in 1984, we went to the canal a couple of times during the summer. At that time I began to fish Vallensbæl in København, where I caught loads of grass carp up to 5kg (11lb), using sweetcorn.

*Was this the only bait that you were using at that time? The same as Lammefjord?*

Yes, sweetcorn, breadpaste and crust with normal sliding leads or freelining. We did a lot of night fishing. I used 'bobbins' directly on the line and silver paper, etc., watching the indicators all the time. Then in the autumn, I did a lot of training for some matches on Vallensbæk, and I was seeing carp, big carp, up to 10kg and I was keen to try and catch one of them. I saw them jumping and rolling so I started to fish more on ledger tackle with sweetcorn and baiting up for long periods.

At that time I started to read other books. I saw 'Carp Fever' for the first time in 1984 and 'Modern Specimen Hunting'. They weren't my books and I only had a quick glance at a friend's copy.

I was at a match in Vallensbæk that year and I tried to fish for carp with light line - much too light line! I managed to catch a 5.2kg carp and then I was very, very keen! I fished on, and one hour later I hooked a carp which stripped almost all the line off the reel and I fought for that fish for - and this is not exaggerated - 1 hour and 20 minutes! It was quite light tackle and I got it to the net, but we didn't have any net that was big enough! A lot of people were gathered round to see what was going on. It was a mirror carp. I still don't know, but I think it was about…over 30lb., between 13½ and 14½kg.

*How many big carp had you seen before, at this time?*

I had seen pictures of them. I had caught cod up to 14kg and I was convinced that this carp was over 30lb. I was still fishing corn and bread.

*When was the time that you first actually used more 'modern' methods?*

Boilies? Yes, well I don't need to say that I lost that carp and I kept dreaming about it for a whole month, and feeling really bad, so I decided that I was going to catch that carp! I started using boilies in the autumn of 1984, and that was cat food/liver paste boilies.

*Were these successful at all?*

Yes. I baited up for a whole week and then fished day and night, and caught a 10.65 kilo mirror, which was the biggest caught in the lake at the time. I was alone; none of the others wanted to put in that much time. Actually, I forgot to mention that I caught an 8kg and a 9.6kg common, poaching a little pool near København. Some of the others fished here when we discovered the pool. They were all commons and we were using bread paste and flake.

*What pool was this?*

It was a **very** private water!

*I think if the readers knew what water it was, they would burst out laughing.* (Jens laughs). *Let's just say that it's close to royalty.* (Jens laughs more!).

Then I concentrated on Vallensbæk after catching that 10kg fish. I spent a lot of time after that first fish, catching nothing!

*Weeks, months … years?*

Years almost! Well, the first time we really started carping was 84 and the next year I did catch some carp in Lammefjord, but nothing big at all.

In 85 I concentrated on big crucians. I caught a lot of crucians up to 1.95kg. The Danish record at that time was 2kg exactly, so this was only 50 grams under the record.

In 86 I fished a lot for bream and I caught bream up to 4kg in Sjæland. In a little lake in a wood we found some big bream and caught about six or seven over 7lb. During these years I left carp alone; I tried a little, but I didn't catch anything.

I almost gave up, but in 87 I had a really strong feeling to catch a big carp, so I went to Jutland because I'd talked to some guys who'd caught some carp in Viborg lake and I decided to go there. I went there for two weeks; I baited up day and night and fished for a week, catching nothing. There were dogs and joggers everywhere and music all night long, and dancing, so I decided to try another water. I left some of my gear with a boy whom I'd met at the lake and took some gear (sleeping bag, bait, etc.) with me and hitchhiked with all this gear on my back to a lake many kms away. I'd heard about the water from a friend; I caught some carp up to 7kg and then went back to Viborg for 1½ weeks and caught only one 4kg fish, down at the lily bay.

I had, up to this time, been used to quite large waters of 60-100 acres like Vallensbæk, and the Viborg lakes are also large, but this new water was much smaller and I really liked that - it made everything feel more intense and closer to the fish. This really gave me back the fever for carp fishing.

I did some fishing for bream on Simsted river in Jutland and caught a lot of bream up to 10lb with fifteen over 8lb.

At Christmas in 1987, I decided to try and catch my first winter carp. I'd caught carp in November but wanted to catch a 'true' winter carp. I went to the small water again on Jutland and I caught a 10kg and 9.8kg (both over 20lb) on float fished flake, and also a smaller 5kg fish - all mirrors.

*So now we're into 1988. What happened in this year?*

This guy called Tony Davies-Patrick (who's he?!) called me. I went over to see him and fished a lake on Fyn. Tony told me that he'd had a 29½ pounder from Kingspool and I went and fished that same water with him. We caught nothing over three days, although Tony hooked a 'biggie' and stripped off naked in the freezing water to try and free the line from a snag, but eventually lost it. We went to some other lakes on Fyn and had a lot of 20's. My best that year from Fyn was 25½lb+ and I had some carp back home at Vallensbæk/Tueholm lakes up to just under 23lb.

*When did you first become interested in Sweden?*

I went to Sweden in 1988 for three weeks, carried out a heavy baiting campaign and caught nothing! This was a water in the Skåne area of about 60 acres. I fished some small waters and caught some carp up to 17½lb. A friend did manage to land a 20lb+ fish from the larger water during the trip. The following year I did some more fishing on Fyn and caught some more 20lb+ carp with Tony.

*You had a second trip to Sweden during this year (1989) with Jesper Petersen; can you tell us more about that?*

We decided to go again because we had heard of some other waters in a completely different area, quite a distance from the lake we had fished in 1988. We drove through Sweden in a large car filled with thousands of boilies! We'd actually visited this water the previous year and although we saw no carp, it looked 'carpy', so we decided to give it a go in 1989. We made up 10,000 boilies before we left and fished two very big waters of maybe 500 acres each. We went in July and decided no matter what, we'd stay the whole month in Sweden.

*Did you have a look around, or did you know a place to go?*

Well, we spent the first three days just looking around this lake in the pouring rain and during the first two days we didn't see anything. We walked during the day and had a good sleep after a bottle of wine at night.

*No fishing at all during those three days? You didn't even wet a line?*

No, although we plumbed the depth in various parts of the lake to get an idea of how deep it was and how fast the bottom sloped off etc., then on the third day of looking there was quite a good wind blowing across a swim that we were standing in. We stood there talking, then suddenly a common of about 15kg or so, crashed out of the water about 20 metres out and, well, then we got a feeling that this might be the swim that we were going to fish first! We started to bait up there; we made an initial bait-up of about 800 boilies and 12 tins of sweetcorn.

*How big were your boilies?*

About 30mm in diameter; quite big ones. We were using Geoff Kemp's Dairy Cream flavour and milk protein based boilies. Later, in fact, we saw another fish jumping in the other lake and so we decided to bait up both swims. We baited these swims very heavily during the next week and in the meantime fished a little pond in a wood and caught only one fish - a fully scaled mirror of about 5kg. The rest of the time was spent making more boilies and then after we had been baiting for a week we decided to fish the first swim.

*What was the reason why you didn't fish the big lake during this week?*

Because we could just as well leave it until the baiting campaign started to work. The bait may have worked straight away, but that's just the way we felt about doing it. Also, because we still had to make a lot of boilies and we spent all day making baits at a friend's house, we were too tired to make any big trips down to the lake and decided to wait.

After the first week, we started to fish but had caught no fish after 6 days. We were fishing with boilie hookbaits over a carpet of boilies and sweetcorn. The first 10 days we actually baited heavily with sweetcorn, but we started to have trouble with roach and line bites, so during the second week we dropped the corn and fished with boilies only. Then one night it was blowing up a very strong wind against the bank and it was pouring down with rain. It was a strong, mild wind from the S/SE. We talked together and said, "Now we've got to get a carp in this weather".

Five minutes after casting the baits out, Jesper got the first run and hooked a 13.3 kilo mirror (29¾lb). A very long, lean, beautiful mirror. I must admit that I was quite green, seeing that fish! We sacked the fish then an hour later I landed a 13 kilo fish (28½lb).

*You were quite pleased by then?*

Yes, ha ha. We were dreaming about this - we were so happy. This had really made our trip and we could have gone home quite happy after this.

When we went over there, we said that if we just caught a carp over the 'Braxendorf' record at 12.4 kilos, we would be more than happy for the rest of our lives! Then the next night it was very clear, with a full moon and I said, "Jesper, we're going to get nothing tonight".

In the middle of the night, around one o' clock, I had a take and landed a 14.3 kilo mirror (31½lb) and I was over the moon! I was just sitting there, feeling happy and then an hour later I got another run and it was a fantastic feeling. On the first run, it took about 100 metres of line (0.35mm) at great speed; I tried to stop it but I couldn't do anything. Suddenly I could see the fish very far out on the surface and it was snagged in a tree or something under the water. I couldn't get it free no matter how I tried, so I gave it 'freeline' to see if if would come free and after a couple of minutes it pulled clear. I then played it **really** hard because I didn't want it to snag again. After quarter of an hour it came closer and made some shorter runs; just as it was beginning to get light Jesper got the fish in the net.

*How long did it take to land?*

Sometimes your judgement of time is lost, but when I hooked the fish it was still dark, in the early hours of dawn and when I got it to the net it was light, so it must have been over half an hour. When Jesper got it into the net he said that he wished that he had his brown trousers on!

When we lifted it onto the bank and unfolded the net, we could see that it was a common carp and it was incredibly big.

*Did you have any idea as to what it might weigh?*

The only thing I could guess was that it must be over 15-16kg (35lb+); I didn't dare guess! Then we discovered that we only had 15 kilogram weighing scales and we became panicky; we tried to parallel two sets of scales and with this arrangement we managed to weigh the fish at around 18kg. We then decided to weigh the fish properly, so we drove all the way to a guy we knew who had 20 kilo scales.

We arrived at 6 o' clock in the morning, throwing boilies at his window and he eventually came down. He went a little pale when we told him that our 15 kilo scales were not enough! The blood slowly came back, to colour his cheeks, and he kindly gave us his own weighing scales.

*Did he come back down to the lake with you?*

No, because he was going to work that day, so we went back to the lake and weighed the fish and it pulled the scales down to 18.4kg (40½lb). We also measured

*Sunrise on a Scandinavian lake.*

*Sunset turns the Twente Canal on fire.*
*Johnny Jensen with a superb grass carp.*

*Left. Jens Larsen with a golden grass carp from Tueholm Lake.*

*Below. Sunrise at Tueholm Lake, Denmark.*

*Many Swedish lakes have a luxuriant weed growth – giving ample food for big fish. Below. Ulf Hansen (centre) with a 24½lb zander, Fleming Madsen (left) and Carsten Gilder (right) are both holding upper doubles. Haralsted Lake, Denmark.*

the fish at 90cms (35$^1/_2$ inches). I was over the moon! On the way back I almost drove into a train!

We drove back to deliver the weights to the guy the same day and, of course, when something fantastic happens, there has to be a contrast - just after we delivered the weights back, my car 'cracked'; I couldn't drive any longer, couldn't move to the side, couldn't do anything, couldn't turn, so we had to have it towed to an auto-repair garage. We found that it would be too expensive to repair so we had the car scrapped and squashed in a mangler! So now we didn't have a car - that was a problem and we decided to hire one.

*Up till now what type of rigs and methods had you been using?*

We were using mostly double balanced boilies with a basic sliding ledger tackle and Drennan boilie hooks, size 2. We used **very** big boilies balanced by a small floater to give it almost neutral buoyancy so that it would sink very, very slowly.

The next night was also an incredible night, I caught a 15.5kg (34lb) mirror and Jesper caught a beautifully scaled 11.2kg (24$^1/_2$lb) mirror.

We then had a couple of days catching nothing, although we didn't care. *(we both started laughing here).* Then I caught a 13.8 kilo mirror (30lb+), followed by another couple of days catching nothing. We then decided to try to fish the other swim on the other lake.

The first night in the new swim I think Jesper caught a 14.4 kilo (31$^1/_2$lb+) mirror, and a carp around 17-19lb which we didn't bother to weigh. The next night I caught a 11.9 (26lb+) mirror and a 9 kilo (19$^3/_4$lb) common.

The following night Jesper landed a 16.6 kilo mirror carp (36$^1/_2$lb+). That was a really incredible fish; he had to jump into the water because it was snagged in some fallen trees. It gave a wonderful fight once he had got it free of the branches; he was standing up to his chest in water, fighting that fish. He eventually got it into the landing net and he was almost drowning because he was so heavy with the water inside his suit and he couldn't lift the fish. I helped him on to the bank and he looked like a Michelin man, with all this water spurting out of his suit.

*Jesper was quite happy by then?*

Yes, Jesper was **quite** happy by that time! The next day I think I caught a 30lb mirror. We fished two more nights and we caught nothing, so we decided to move to yet another swim which we had started to bait up.

*This was in the same lake?*

Yes, the second lake. We decided to move and it was quite a pity for Jesper because we had bet each other who was going to deliver the car back to the car-rent, and I won the bet so I went down to the lake alone, carrying all the gear. I started to fish…

When Jesper came back, he saw my sack in the water and asked…

*How long had he been away?*

He'd been away two hours… and he asked, "What's in the sack?"

*Jens demonstrates the potential of Sweden and Denmark with these two brace of twenties – one from each country.*

I said, "Which of them?"

He went quite pale! I'd caught a 13.5 kilo (29¾lb) and a 13.3 kilo (29¼lb), both mirrors.

*This was while he was away? I bet he was cheesed off?*

Yes, just a little! We fished that night and Jesper had a 22lb+ mirror, for which he had to wade out in the water again, so that he could get if free of some snags. That pleased him a bit, catching that fish.

We stayed there for another 3 days; I think the only other fish we caught was an 11 kilo (24lb+) beautiful, pale coloured mirror. By that time we had been in Sweden for a month, so now we were missing home and a clean bath and everything, so we decided to head for home.

We were quite pleased with our trip and decided to say nothing to the members of the D.K.K., before we had made the slide show.

It was quite funny because we said, "Oh, we haven't caught anything much" and when we had the slide show, we were putting the smallest carp in first, and then up in weights. It was quite a noisy gathering of lads watching the slides and drinking beers, with the occasional remark of "not bad" as another, slightly bigger double came up on the screen. As each of the larger carp were 'clicked' through the viewer, the shouting and laughing gradually seeped away and by the end of the evening when the 40½lb common/31½lb brace were shown, you could have heard a pin drop!

*(I started laughing at this point).*

*Thank you Jens. I think the pubs are open and it's your round…*

# Tour of Sweden

Sweden has a fantastic array of rivers and lakes. Many of the lakes are **very** large by English standards, but so are some of the fish! Much of the country is covered by beautiful forests and marshlands, and it is a wonderful country to spend a holiday - just bring your rods and tent and explore…

Sweden is divided into area boundaries, so I will go through each area at a time, naming some of the best waters as I go. Remember, many waters are, as yet, untapped, so once in the area it is advisable to try unknown lakes. If you are not interested in extra large lakes, there is no problem, as there are literally thousands of small lakes and pools to choose from.

We will begin in the south and work our way slowly north. The first area is **Skåne**, just across the water from Denmark.

6km north of Malmö at Lomma is a group of lakes holding good crucians to 3lb+.

To the east of Malmö and 2km south of Genarp is the lovely Häckberga lake with large islands and bays, surrounded by woodlands. This relatively large water has produced bream to $13^3/_4$lb.

Svanholm lake to the south of Hackeberga, near Surup, also holds good crucians to $3^1/_2$lb.

The river Kävling river runs through the large Vamblake near Sjöbo and travels west until it reaches the sea at Bjarred. Just upstream from Bjärred at Löddeköping, is a good place for bream and pike. A number of 20-35lb pike have been caught here with the best an incredible $45^1/_2$lb! The river also holds good carp, especially in the warm water section near Almundagård, with a number of common carp between 15 and 23lb. Tench to $9^1/_2$lb have been caught in the river at Glåms lake section near Örtofa.

The Rönne river runs out of the huge Rings lake at Sätofta and makes its way north through Skåne to the Skalderviken (inlet) at Ängelholm. This is another good bream water with specimens up to 9lb+; the best area is near Klippan, 12km east of Åstorp on route 21.

Just north of the river at Riseberga (near Ljungbyhed) is the Bank lake, holding carp to over 30lb (there has been rumour that acid rain has affected this lake recently). Vinslöv lake, south east of Hässleholm, holds double figure grasscarp up to 15lb. At Vittsjo, 18km north of Hässleholm lies the two Vitt lakes with many carp between 15-20lb. The river Alma is an excellent chub water with some fish over $6^1/_2$lb - the best area is around Hanaskog, 20km north of Kristianstad.

The **Blekinge** area is dominated by that famous salmon water - the river Mörrum, which runs between Fridafors and Elleholm, near Mörrum town. This expansive stretch of river holds salmon to over 50lb and sea trout to over 32lb! Start opening your wallet!

The Ronneby river contains good bream and pike at Kallinge and Möljeryd. 25km east of Ronneby on the E66, lies the large town of Karlskrona. The area off the coast between Karlskrona and the Hasslö, Aslpö, Tjurkö, Sturkö island belt is a wonderful area for pike. Here many big fish roam amongst the archipelago (in Sweden these shallow island clusters off the coast are known as Skärgårds), with numbers of 25-35lb pike caught every year, with some reaching 40lb! Large powan are also caught at the SaltöFiskhamn to 10lb.

*Stig Nilsson with a giant sea trout of 31¹/₂lb from the River Em.*

71

*The lake and river complexes of Sweden in greater detail. See main map on Page 70.*

The Lyckby river holds good bream, roach, tench, pike and many eels over 4lb, with some specimens reaching 7lb+. One of the best areas is where the river runs through the lake system to the north of Karlskrona at Kattilsmåla.

Another good area of the river is at Vissefjarda in Småland. We have now moved into the **Småland** area, which is one of the best in Sweden. 25km east of Vissefjärda, just past Påryd; the 120 road runs alongside the Hagby river. This river holds many big bream between 7-11lb up to $12\frac{1}{2}$lb; rudd to 3lb+ and pike to 31lb!

North east of the Hagby river at Ljungbyholm is the Ljungby river (11km SW of Kalmar on the E66). This wonderful river contains many tench over 6lb up to 9lb+. The best area is the Kölby dam on the outskirts of the town. Many bream between 8 and $11\frac{1}{2}$lb are also caught here.

Another good place is the Kupagölan, downstream of Hassmo, with carp to 22lb+. Upstream at Trekanten is another good place for large bream and tench.

13km NW of Trekanten, on route 25 at Nybro, lies the Linnea lake with commons to 20lb+ and mirrors to 25lb. North of Kalmar on the E66 coast road we cross the large river Em, just before Emfors. This is Sweden's best catfish river with fish over 132lb landed! Near here, just off the coastline around Påskallavik and Runno island, is good for sea trout between 20 and 25lb+! The best sea trout from the river itself was a fantastic $31\frac{1}{4}$lb!! Up river on the Em is good for chub to over 5lb, especially at Högsby.

*Fehmi Varlis with a huge pike of 57¹/₄lb from Skargarrd.*
*Below: Jens Ploug Hausen battles it out with a tail walking Swedish pike.*

Vaxjö, a large town in central Småland is a good area to base yourself. A very large stretch of water dominates the landscape to the north of the town, called the Helga lake. There are four main arms and hundreds of islands and bays scattered over thousands of acres. The lake contains a host of different species to specimen size, but carp is one of the best known species. A large number of 20-30lb commons swim in this huge lake, but it obviously takes a lot of water watching and large baiting campaigns to find the shoals - but who knows? - common carp to $32^3/_4$lb were turning up amongst many 20's in the early 80's, so anything might turn up in the 90's!

North of Helga lake lies the smaller (8km long!) Straken lake, which also holds good carp. Drive north on route 30 then turn left on route 126 to Lidnow, or drive 5km further north and turn off towards Aneboda to reach the northern end of the lake. The large Kronoberg lake has turned up carp to $29^1/_2$lb.

A number of smaller lakes in the area also hold carp and this is a good area to explore, especially around Berg, Tolg and Bergkvara. The Bergund lake south of Vaxjo contains crucians to 3lb+.

The river which runs into the Salen lake near Gamla (west of Vaxjo) holds chub to 5lb+ but the river that runs out of the Salen into the Skatelov holds even better chub with some fish landed over $6^1/_2$lb. Drive SW on route 23 from Vaxjo and the road crosses the river at Huseby village. The Salen lake itself holds carp over 33lb. The Skatelov lake runs into the huge Åsnen lake which has produced big pike and zander to 20lb amongst many other species.

In the south western corner of Småland lies the town of Markaryd (12km north of Vittsjon on route 117). The small Skars lake near this town holds double figure grass carp, common carp to upper doubles and mirrors over 20lb. The Ands lake also holds good common carp. The Helge river, 11km west of Älmhult on route 120 at Delary, holds good zander to over $14^1/_2$lb, especially where the river runs into the Delary lake.

The massive Bolmen lake makes the Helga lake look 'puny' and lies west of Ljungby. It holds big pike and zander to over $17^1/_2$lb. The best area is around Lillaryd and Sparda at the NE end or from the Bolm island. Another decent zander water is situated just east of Bolmen. Take route 127 SE from Värnmo and then turn east at Bar towards Gällaryd. 3km after Gällaryd, turn right on south road for 5km to where the road crosses the junction of the Lynen and Hulta lakes. Both lakes hold zander into upper doubles.

North west of Värnamo, past Hillestorp and just south of Marieholm, is Moss lake. This lovely looking water with many bays and two major islands, is about 495 acres and holds pike between 20-30lb.

The upper reaches of the Em river (remember those catfish downstream?), at Adelfors on route 127 east of Vetlanda is a good area for chub to 6lb+. 24km north of Vetlanda on route 31 at Stensjon, lies the Nömmon lake. This 9km long, 3km wide stretch of water contains many islands and it is better to use a boat to cover the numerous 'pikey' looking haunts. The 'esox' itself grows to over 30lb in this lake, with many over 20lb.

14km further north at Nässjo, lies the Runseryds lake with good roach between $1^1/_2$-$2^1/_2$lb and Ingberg lake, which is a good tench water with specimens to 7lb+.

Turning north off route 31, just after Forserum and driving through

Lekeryd and Svärttop, we come to the 6km long Ylen lake, containing big zander to over 20lb! The lower Store Näteren lake also produces big zander, with some over 15lb.

Turning off route 132 at Haurida and driving north past Ruppen lake, we come to the large Bunn lake. This is one of Sweden's best pike waters with many big fish up to 35lb+. The northern side of the lake opens out and holds many islands and features.

A few km to the east at Hultrum village is the 7km long Ören lake with the town of Oserum on its northern shoreline. This water, as well as holding large pike, has produced char to over 19lb! SE of Ören, between Friiaryd and Areby is the 6km long Ralången lake. This is a good zander water, with the best at 20½lb and numerous fish into double figures. The Svart river, which runs out of the northern end and flows through Säby lake, is a good chub river.

By driving directly east across Småland from Nässjo on route 33, we come to the east coast at Västervik. 12km before Västervik at Gunnebo, is the Verkebäcksviken (viken = inlet or small fjord). This inlet has produced a number of pike to 32lb. The Skärgård, off the coast between Vastervik and Loftahammer, has also produced a number of big pike to over 30lb. The Kaggbfjord to the north of Lofthammer at Östra Ed is a wonderful area for big perch, with numerous specimens over 4½lb. A ferry regularly goes between Västervik and Visby on Gotland island. One of the best places lies 28km south of Visby near Västergarn. Just north of town at the village of Sigvards, the river Wästergarn runs through a lake where crucians have been caught to almost 5½lb! It also holds rudd to over 3lb.

We now move into the **Halland** district, which runs along the west coast. Perch to 3lb+ can be found in the lake just north of Våxtorp on route 24. An even better proposition for big perch is further north to the river Lagan. The best area is just south of Kattarp, where the river runs through a series of backwaters, including the adjoining Store lake. Perch have been caught in the backwaters to over 4½lb and many other species make good weights.

The Ätran river provides good mixed fishing for big pike, roach, chub, etc., at Vessigebro, NE of Falkenberg.

5km east of Vessigebro is the Sjönevad lake. The water covers 300 acres, including a smaller southern bay and holds many bream to over 8lb and large eels. Upstream of Vessigebro the river is better known as the Högvards river and at Svartra village salmon have turned up, with some fish over 27lb.

The E6 road leaves Halland at Lindome and enters the **Väster Gotland** district at Göteborg. This city is probably the first port of call for many of you arriving by ferry and will be of primary interest. I'll try my best to guide you to the best waters, lads!

15km east of Göteborg on the E3 at Aspen/Lerum is the 4½km long Aspen lake - a good zander water with specimens to 17½lb and 20lb+ pike.

Further NE on the E3 at Västra Bodarne/Alingsas is the huge Mjorn lake which has produced trout to over 21lb! The best area for bream over 8lb is at the Säva inlet near Norsesund, south of Västra. The river Säva above Alingsås holds large asp. The best area is 21km NE on the E3 at Våagårde where specimens over 6¼lb are caught.

The Hars lake, just north of Hyssna, is a first class bream water (drive east from Göteborg on route 40, then turn south on route 156). This lake holds many bream over 9lb with some monsters over 13lb! South of Hyssna at Berghem on route 41 is the river Visk/Häggen which holds good chub to 5lb+.

The Viareds lake, south of Sandared (west of Borås) contains zander to 16½lb.

The Kolbräningen area of lakes near Borås has produced pike to 39½lb!

The Vaster and Bos lakes near Funningen village to the SW of Borås are also very good for pike. Directly 15km south of Borås and 3km east of Kinnarumma is the western arm of Fri lake; the eastern arm runs between Bottnen and Påholmen villages. This is another good zander water with numerous fish over 17 and 18lb, and eels up to 4½lb.

13km SE of here, near Svenlunga, is the small Annlarpa lake at Häcksvick village which holds perch up to 4½lb.

25km east of Borås on route 40, lies the large 10km long Tolken lake, holding good pike, zander and many perch between 2-4lb.

Further east at Ulricehamn is the 14km long Åsmunden lake which runs into the smaller Southern Åsmunden and Torp lakes. This water has produced many big pike and zander.

The Säm lake lies to the east of Annelund (drive north of Borås on route 42/183 to Annelund and then east on route 182 towards Od). This large and wonderful looking water has produced many carp lately over 20lb, with the best landed at 27¾lb; this is a very large lake and I'm sure the biggest have yet to be contacted.

On the southern shore of the huge Vänern (or Dalbo lake), which is more like an ocean, near the town of Vargon where the Göta river leaves the Vänern is a good area for lake trout to over 23lb! The Slump river above Sjuntorp and around the village of Velanda is good for chub to over 5lb. The Nossan river at Nossebro is also good for chub, but usually a little smaller - in the 4-4½lb region.

A better proposition is the Lidan river, which runs from Eriksberg to the Kinneviken bay of the Vänern at Lidkoping. The best areas are at Hälum and Trassberg, with chub reaching 6¼lb. Good chub fishing is also to be had on the upper reaches of the Tiden river between Tibro and Fridene. 6km NE of Tibro, on route 49 at Ransberg, lies the large, crescent shaped Örlen lake. This is a good bream water with many over 8lb.

We now cross over into **ÖsterGotland** district and begin in the south at Österbymo on route 134. Svärdstorp lake on the Bulsjo river is good for tench to over 7lb and eels to 3½lb. The Nästangen pool also holds tench to 7lb and good eels, but the best place for really big eels is in the small Österlake just near the outlet to the river, where many specimens over 4lb have been caught, with the best at 6¾lb.

The massive Sommen holds many large species, including lake trout to over 20lb. The best area is in the northern section between Blävick and the Svart river. The Svart river itself holds good chub all along its length, with the best areas at Normlosa, where the river runs into a 3km long, narrow lake. Here chub are caught to over 5½lb, roach to 2½lb and bream to 8lb. Further downstream, the river runs into another pool near Alvested, holding large rudd to 3lb+. Further downstream still, between Ledberg and Kaya, bream to 10lb and big rudd have turned up in the large pools. The river also holds big eels, with specimens to over

*Idyllic surroundings on a Swedish lake.*

*A boat is essential on many of the bigger Swedish waters.*

8lb landed near Mjolby.

The large Åsunden lake system between Horn and Rumforsa (east of Kisa), contains many big fish, including zander to 19½lb. The large Bråviken inlet cuts deep into the east coast at Norreköping. If you thought that the Åsunden zander were big, then get a load of this - zander to an incredible 26½lb have been landed in the Braviken!!

The smaller Slälbaken to the south, at Skallvik, also produces monster zander, including big pike. The Ned Längas lake to the east of Kisa has produced eels to 5lb+.

We now cross the Bråviken and enter the **SöderManland** district at Nykoping. 37km NE, on the E4, and 6km south on the 218, lies the town of Trosa. The coastal waters in the area (Trosa Skärgård) are hot spots for big zander and large pike to 39½lb!

Stockholm's Skärgård is another wonderful area for big pike, with a fantastic array of islands. One of the best areas is the Ljustero islands and around the Yzlan/Blido islands. Many 30-35lb+ pike are landed each year, including sea trout up to 20lb, large zander, roach, rudd and perch. Crucians to 4lb+ have been caught on the Inner island.

The Stora Värtan inlet at Näsby on northern Stockholm's outskirts, produces many 5lb+ eels every year. The Babäken lake at Häringe, near the coast, 10km south of Hanginge on the 73 road from Stockholm, contains big crucians to 4lb. Large crucians can also be caught in Öringe lake, a 1,600 metre long stretch of water at Öringe on the 224 (Tyresövagen) SE of Stockholm. Turn off on the Vårvagen, then left on Stumnäsvägen, to reach this lovely looking water.

*Zander flourish in many Swedish Lakes.*
*The Ljungby River holds big tench. This lovely specimen (below) was caught by Tony.*

Another nice looking water lies in a wooded park in the Djursholm area of Stockholm. From Djursholm/Ösby train station, walk along Vendervägen, then left along Fafnervägen. This 300 metre long, 200 metre wide lake holds many grass carp into double figures, leather carp over 22lb and commons to 28lb.

In the Torbyfjord at Gustavserg (east of Stockholm on route 74), pike have been caught to 38½lb. Big powan (whitefish) to 8lb are caught at Galo (south on route 73). The very large Mäleren, to the west of Stockholm, holds big asp to 12¾lb. The best area is the inlet at Mälhammer, a few km east of Kvicksund. Pike to an incredible 49½lb have been caught in the Vasteras inlet, part of the Mäleren around Almo-Lindo (Västermanland). The best areas for zander over 15lb are the Görvaln, and Lamberfjarden at Hässelby. Just off the E3, west of Stockholm, near Nykvarn, lies the Vidby lake holding crucians to 4¼lb.

In the southern **Dalsland** district near Torp, 20km north on route 172 from Uddevalla, lies the Elleno lake. This is a good eel water with a number over 4½lb. A great many carp between 20lb and 34½lb have been caught at a particular lake in Dalsland near Uddevalla, but its precise location still escapes me!

Another good place for eels lies to the north, just over the border into **Varmland** district, near Saffle. Close to where the river runs out of the Harefjord to the north of town is good for specimens to 5lb+. The E45, north of Saffle, takes us to Karlstad. 22km north of town, near Forshaga, is the Skarva lake which contains many crucians between 3-4lb+ and tench to 6½lb.

A good crucian water lies in the **Vastermanland** district, 20km north of Vasterås at Svanå, called the Hälls lake. Specimens to over 4½lb have been landed here, including good chub. Large asp to just under 17lb have been taken in the river running down between Skinnskatteberg and Kolsva.

We now move east into the **Uppland** district. South of Uppsala is the large Ekoln lake. This is a very good zander water, with many between 10-18lb. The best area is off the Vrela point, near the entrance to the Dalby arm. The Fyri river, to the north of Uppsala, at Storvreta is good for rudd over 2lb and ide to 6½lb.

Further north on the 290 road at Dannemora, is the 3km long Gruv lake, which is good for many species, including large roach. Some fantastic rudd have been caught in the Strand lake to almost 5lb! Where is this water you ask? - 3km south of Järlåsa on route 72, west of Uppsala.

Off the east coast at Rådmansö, east of Norrtälje, is a good spot for large pike to 30lb+. 24km north of Norrtälje, at Blocka, is the long Skebaruk lake which holds crucians to 4½lb. Further north on the 76 road at Östhammar is also very good for large pike to 36½lb and zander to 15lb+. The favourite area is around Tvärnö and the Värling island.

Further north on the 76 road at Gävle in **Gästrikland** is the Gavle river. This is another good rudd water, with some over 3½lb. At the southern tip of Gastrikland, near Gysinge, is the Edsviken (the central section of the Hedesunda-Färnab lake system). Here is a good area for large pike, and zander over 16lb.

We cross east now, into the **Dalarna** district. Just east of Ludvika on the 65 road is the 3km long Ned. Hillen lake. This is a very good 'sergeant' water, with some truly monster perch up to 5¾lb. The Bys lake and the adjoining Bjorken lake hold trout to 20lb+, good pike, and perch to 4½lb. There are a number of surrounding smaller lakes situated at Grangärde, 20km north of Ludvika on route 247, which also provide good sport. Crucians to 4½lb can be caught in the Östenfors river pools near Falum (route 80). The large 14km wide Ti lake on the winding road west of Limedsfarsen (turn left off route 297 at Ärnas) holds pike to 27lb+. 18km north of Salen on route 297 lies the beautiful Harrmunden lake, probably one of the most northerly lakes in Europe holding big bream, with specimens over 9½lb.

One exceptional eel water lies in the southern part of **Hälsingland** district, 5km SE of Holmsreden near Vastby village. The Vastby lake has turned up monster 'bootlaces' (eels) to 8¼lb!

One of the best areas in the **Ångermanland** district to base yourself, is near the east coast at Örnskoldsvik. The Stroms river system contains many large ide between 5lb and 6½lb and numerous bream over 8lb, up to 10lb+. Large sea trout (best at night) to over 19½lb can be caught in the Ångerman river; one of the better areas is close to Sollefteå on route 90.

We now move into the wild and desolate **Jamtland** district. The incredible Stor lake system provides wonderful sport with large lake trout. One of the best areas is the 4km long Äcklingen lake, just 3km north of the huge Kall lake near Kolåsen village. You can expect to latch on to trout over 22lb! Further north, at Strömsund, stretches the impressive Ströms Vattudal lake system - very large pike, perch and trout swim in its wild and beautiful waters.

We finish our tour of Sweden in **Lappland**, among the reindeer. The Ume river/lake system is the best area to head for, for trout. The Storaman lake on route E79 (the polar circle road!), just north of Storaman town, holds trout in excess of 27lb! Large powan are to be found in Lappland. Two of the best areas are the Konkämä river that runs along the Swedish/Finnish border, and in the Kummaeno tributary at Kummaruopio village, where specimens to over 9lb can be caught.

Oh, I nearly forgot - Keith Barker and Dave Tipping will never forgive me if I don't mention burbot! In the large Lule river, near Boden in the **Norrebotten** district, just south of Lappland, burbot have been landed to almost 15lb!

Obviously the Swedes don't fish the river Rother...

# Norway's Best Coarse Fishing Waters

## By

## Inge Christopher Solberg
## and friends

**GENERAL**

Norway is a country with more than 250,000 lakes and ponds and an unknown number of rivers and streams, altogether offering rich possibilities for freshwater fishing.

The main interest of angling is concentrated around species like salmon, sea trout, trout, char, grayling, pike and perch. The remaining species and especially the cyprinids are totally neglected by most. For the few serious coarse anglers in Norway (not more than 150!!), this leaves a wealth of possibilities.

Although Norway is a large country, with a lot of remote and wild areas, the most interesting coarse angling fisheries can be found in the more populated areas in the south of the country, where distances are moderate and access is good.

In the following, only the coarse fishing of Norway is described; trout and salmon fishing is not covered to any extent, except where good coarse fishing can be found in salmon rivers. For general information on angling in Norway, the book 'A Guide to Angling in Norway' can be obtained from most bookshops. The book covers the whole of Norway, including close seasons, fishing licences, camp sites etc. As the authors of that book considered that the interest for coarse fishing in Europe is as low as in Norway, they have completely left out the regions described in the following pages.

For the following rivers and lakes there is normally no need for a fishing licence. There is, however, a regulation saying that everyone has to pay a general fee to the State Fishing Fund in order to fish for fresh water fish in Norway. This licence can be obtained from any post office and costs 110 NOK (1990) a year. If in doubt, ask the landowner for permission.

In the following, only a small number of rivers and lakes are described. These are well known to the authors and have offered excellent sport over the years. Access is, in most cases, good and the areas can offer a good selection of camping sites etc. Other lakes and rivers in the south and southeast of Norway can probably offer just as good fishing, as the true potential is far from known.

One good piece of advice is to bring most of your coarse fishing gear with you when visiting Norway. In most towns proper floats, leads, hooks, rods, groundbait etc., cannot be bought. If salmon, trout and pike spinning gear is what you are looking for, there are no problems, most tackle shops stock them. Also, bring your own maggots and casters as they can hardly be bought and if they can, the prices are sky high.

## THE COURSE OF HALDEN AND ITS TRIBUTARIES.

### Location

This watercourse has got its name from the small town HALDEN at the outlet. The course of Halden is located in the county of Østfold, close to the Swedish border. The watercourse consists mainly of one river, TISTA (1) and a lot of quite large lakes, FEMSJØEN (2), ASPEREN (3), AREMARKSJØEN (4), RØDENESSJØEN (5), HEMNESSJØEN (6), RØMSJØEN (7), SETTEN (8) AND BJØRKELANGEN (9). There are also quite a few small lakes.

### Fish stocks

All the rivers and lakes are stocked with perch, pike and roach.

The perch grow to quite a large size - in fact, 5 pounders occur! Usually the perch grow to 2-3lb but there are hordes of small ones to get through in order to catch the bigger ones.

Pike grow to large sizes in nearly all the rivers and lakes. Pike to 15-20lb are quite normal, especially in the lakes. The maximum is 30lb+.

The roach only grow to a small size.

The Halden watercourse is also stocked with a lot of other species; bream, white bream, rudd, chub, crucian carp, bleak, zander, burbot and eel. Zander and chub occur only near the outlet. Eel are not a common species, but almost every eel which is caught is large (in excess of 3lb). The bream is common and can grow to more than 10lb. Rudd to 1lb is quite normal with a potential of 2lb+.

In a couple of lakes (especially BJØRKELANGEN) there's a good possibility of big bags of fish (bream to 4lb, rudd to 2lb and scores of small roach, white bream and bleak).

### Access.

The fishing in the HALDEN watercourse is mostly free. Access can be difficult at places, due to enormous reed beds. This is a problem, especially in HEMNESSJØEN, probably the best lake for bream in the whole watercourse.

Wherever you are going it would be advantageous to bring a boat or canoe, especially on the larger lakes.

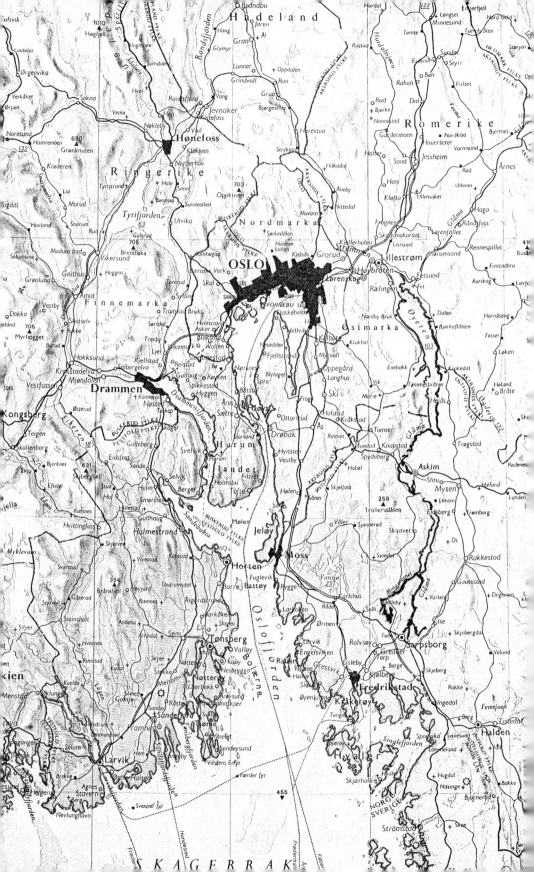

# THE LOWER PART OF GLOMMA RIVER.

## Location.

The lower part of river GLOMMA (10) runs from the lake ØYEREN (covered under ROMERIKE) south east of Oslo and ends in the town of Fredrikstad 90km south of Oslo. 15km north of the town Sarpsborg, GLOMMA splits and follows two different courses which join just south of Sarpsborg. The main, easterly course runs through the lake GLENGSHØLEN (11), while the westerly course runs through the lakes MINGEVANNET (12) and VESTVANNET (13) prior to changing name to river ÅGÅRDSELVA (14). ÅGÅRDSELVA runs through the lake VISTERFLO (15) to join the easterly GLOMMA course. Also located in this area are the lakes TUNEVANNET (16) and ISESJØEN (17).

## Fish Stocks.

In general, it can be said that this part of GLOMMA and its lakes can offer some of the most exciting coarse fishing in Norway. The area is far from fully explored, and in the following, only the most popular areas are covered (popular does not, in this context, mean crowded).

The species available are asp (not known in the British Isles), ide, chub, roach, rudd, bream, silver bream, dace, grayling, houting, burbot, eel, pike, zander and trout, as well as sea trout and salmon.

*A large ide in the landing net. Norway is a paradise for big ide.*

*Rolf Berge with two good tench
from Lake Jovann
© Inge Solberg.*

*Rune Johansen with a 6lb 2oz
chub from the River Glomma,
upstream of the power station
at Sarpsborg. © I.C. Solberg.*

River ÅGÅRDSELVA, north of Solli Bridge (where the E6 from Oslo crosses the river) is not open for coarse fishing unless you buy a licence for salmon fishing.

The stretch from Solli Bridge, south to VISTERFLO, offers free and excellent fishing. In early spring, large bags of bream averaging 2-3lb can be caught, but in late May through to September, the main interest is concentrated around the chub fishing. Bags of 20 chub in a session are nothing unusual, with an average size of about 2lb. The maximum size is probably 7lb, but 6lb+ fish are caught every year. In addition, rudd to 2lb, pike to 25lb and zander to 15lb can be caught. Lake VISTERFLO is best known for its perch, pike and zander. In this lake the perch runs to 6lb!

A 'hot spot' during June, July, August and September is the stretch of GLOMMA upstream of the power station in the town of Sarpsborg. Chub and ide to 6lb+ are caught here every season - probably Norway's best stretch for specimen ide. The fishing is vulnerable to water level, but July and August are normally quite safe.

Another 'hot spot' for chub is the stretch downstream of the VAMMA power station, some 20km south of lake ØYEREN. The locations mentioned here are the ones most frequently visited by coarse anglers, but any swim along this huge river can turn up big surprises. The true potential of GLOMMA as a pike river is not known as there is only a handful of really serious pike anglers in the region, but fish to 30lb+ are caught every year.

### Access.

Access to the river bank can be difficult at places, but in the areas mentioned above, plenty of swims are available.

The fishing is free, apart from the salmon stretch in river ÅGÅRDSELVA, north of Solli Bridge.

## THE COURSE OF MOSS AND ITS TRIBUTARIES

### Location.

The watercourse has got its name from the town MOSS at the outlet. The course of MOSS is positioned in the middle of the county of Østfold. The watercourse consists of one large lake, VANSJØ (18), a couple of small rivers HOBØLELVA (19), FLESJØELVA (20) and a couple of smaller lakes SÆBYVANNET (21) and FLESJØVANNET (22).

### Fish stocks.

The large lake VANSJØ is stocked with a lot of species, and the most important are, pike, zander, perch, eel, rudd, bream and roach. The lake is very exciting; it contains a lot of small sounds, bays and islands; there are lots of swims. It is advantageous to use a boat, at least to move between swims. The pike, zander, perch and rudd all grow to good sizes. The maximum weight for eels in this lake is as much as 7-8lb.

HOBØLELVA has its outlet in the northern part of Vansjø. This river has chub to 4lb. In the stretches near the outlet there are perch, pike, zander and rudd of good sizes.

FLESJØELVA is a very small river which has its outlet in the eastern part of Vansjø. The river has a couple of nice pools, which are stocked with bream to 7-8lb. In the small lakes of FLESJØVANNET and SÆBYVANNET there are also bream to 7-8lb. These small lakes are also stocked with millions of small roach and rudd. Big rudd can be found, the maximum size probably being between 2 and 3lb. These small lakes are also stocked with some very large eels.

### Access.

The fishing is mostly free but bear in mind that parts of this area are prohibited to foreigners for military reasons.

All the lakes in the area have large reed and weed beds, but good swims can be found.

## ROMERIKE

### Location.

Romerike is the central part of the county of AKERSHUS. The main watercourse is GLOMMA, as well as its tributaries NITELVA (24), LEIRA (25), VORMA (26) and the large lake ØYEREN (27).

### Fish stocks.

The lake ØYEREN is the Norwegian lake which is stocked with the largest quantity of species - 24! The most important species are, pike, perch, zander, burbot, bream, ide, chub, roach, houting, grayling, dace, white bream and bleak.

In terms of angling, the ØYEREN lake has tremendous potential. It contains pike to 40lb (!!) and twenties are quite normal. The perch grow to about 6lb (!!) but the normal size is between 1 and 2lb. The lake holds a fair amount of really large burbot up to 15lb!

The ØYEREN lake is very large, and for this reason bank fishing is not that effective; a boat is almost a necessity.

Every year, nearly all the species in the ØYEREN migrate for spawning; the fish migrate to the rivers GLOMMA, NITELVA AND LEIRA.

GLOMMA is famous for its large burbot, especially the area near the lake ØYEREN. Your best chances are as early as January and February - during cold winters it is tradition to fish burbot from the ice!

The river GLOMMA also has great potential for pike (to 30lb). Glomma is also stocked with the most common species, perch, grayling, trout, ide, bream, roach etc., and most of the species grow to a nice size.

The river NITELVA has its outlet in the north west corner of lake ØYEREN, near the village of Lillestrøm. During March and April, pike fishing is very popular and pike to 30lb+ are caught every season. The stretches close to Lillestrøm also hold large shoals of bream to 3lb, ide to 4lb+, small roach and white bream, as well as billions of small bleak.

In the upper parts of the river NITELVA there is the possibility of chub, ide and pike to good sizes. The record Norwegian chub was caught in this area back in 1977; it weighed 6lb 9oz. These days it seems that the maximum size of the chub is between 4 and 5lb and 4 pounders don't occur too often - but who knows, maybe there are still chub to 6lb?

The river LEIRA also has its outlet in the lake ØYEREN at Lillestrøm. In May and June the zander fishing can be brilliant but, unfortunately, most of the zander are killed.

VORMA is the name of the river between lake MJØSA and river GLOMMA.

The stretch downstream, SVANFOSSEN (28), can offer good fishing for brown trout to 10-15lb, grayling to 3lb, houting to 3lb and, during the late summer, also scores of ide to 4-5lb.

### Access.

Most of the fishing in this area is free. As mentioned earlier, both lake ØYEREN and river GLOMMA are very large and a boat is a great advantage, but you **can** find swims where you can fish from the bank, especially in the GLOMMA river.

On river NITELVA there are lots of swims and access is very good.

In river LEIRA the access is not so good; almost everywhere there are trees overhanging the bank. Ask the locals for advice and direction.

## MYSENELVA RIVER

### Location.

The MYSENELVA (23) river is a canal like river, located approximately 70km south east of Oslo. The river is small and, in most parts, not more than 4-5m wide.

The river is 'fishable' from the GREFSLIVANN lake, 10km north of the Mysen village, all the way to its outlet in the river GLOMMA.

### Fish stocks.

The MYSENELVA can offer brilliant fishing and huge bags of perch, rudd, bream, roach, white bream, dace and eels. The roach and rudd run to 2lb, whilst the average bream is 3-4lb.

### Access.

Access to the river is good, and a lot of good swims are available. Fishing is free but, if in doubt, ask the landowner for permission.

## AKERSVIKA

### Location.

The AKERSVIKA river delta is located in the town of Hamar some 110km north of Oslo. The E6 from Oslo crosses AKERSVIKA just outside Hamar. The AKERSVIKA is part of Norway's largest lake, MJØSA, famous for its large brown trout.

### Fish stocks.

This river delta is probably Norway's most well known coarse fishery and abounds with huge shoals of bream, roach and ide, as well as large perch and pike. From April to October, nets of fish in excess of 100lb can be taken on either the float or the bomb, with worm, corn or bread. Maggot is also a good bait, but with so many small fish also present, seldom used apart from in matches. The best months for 'bagging up' are April and May, when ide, grouping to head up river to spawn, are caught in large numbers on almost every trip. 60 or more of these fish, averaging 1kg or more, can be taken in just four or five hours' fishing.

Fishing during these two months is limited to certain zones, due to the area being a nature reserve. From June 1st fishing is open (and free) everywhere. From June to October, the bream fishing comes on form with fish up to 8lb (average 3lb) being caught in large numbers.

Interesting also for the pike angler, AKERSVIKA produces pike over 30lb every season, the best months being May, June and July. The roach fishing on this water is also very good, average size about 7oz, with fish over 1lb being rare.

All in all, AKERSVIKA is an excellent fishery where, under all but extreme weather conditions, a 'blank' is an impossibility.

## THE COURSE OF DRAMMEN AND ITS TRIBUTARIES.

### Location.
The DRAMMENSELVA (29) river, TYRIFJORDEN (30) lake and STORELVA (31) river are located in an area stretching from the town of Drammen near the Oslofjord, 40km south west of Oslo, to the town of Hønefoss, some 60km north west of Oslo.

DRAMMENSELVA is Norway's second largest river w.r.t. rate of water flow, while TYRIFJORDEN is one of Norway's larger lakes with an area of 234 square kilometers and a maximum depth of 295 metres!

### Fish stocks.
DRAMMENSELVA, running from TYRIFJORDEN to the town of Drammen, has turned into one of Norway's better salmon rivers in recent years. The salmon fishing is concentrated on the large pool underneath the Hellefossen waterfall at Hokksund. As 99% of all salmon caught, are from this pool, it can be ranked as the best salmon pool in the whole of Norway. (Maybe the best in the world?). The record for Hellefossen is held by a salmon of 76lb (34.5kg), which is the second largest ever caught in Norway.

The slower parts of the river from Hellefossen to Drammen, offer brilliant coarse fishing. Apart from pike to 30lb, the river holds good heads of trout, houting, eel, bream, roach, ide, chub, rudd, perch and crucian carp. Bags of up to 60lb are not uncommon, especially during spring.

TYRIFJORDEN lake, approximately 40km north west of Oslo, offers some of the best fishing in Norway for specimen pike and wild brown trout. Most fishing is done by boat, and in recent years excellent results have been obtained by modern deep-trolling techniques. A number of pike between 20 and 30lb are caught each year, while brown trout in the 7-12lb bracket are not uncommon. The largest trout ever caught in TYRIFJORDEN is said to have been 52lb., but this has never been confirmed.

Apart from pike and trout, the specimen hunter can find good bream and crucian carp fishing in this lake. The true potential is unknown, but bream to 10-11lb are caught every year in nets.

*The possibilities! Inge Solberg and Pete Knight with a 440lb catch of bream (to 5lb) and perch (to 2$^1$/$_2$lb) taken in a morning session at Akerskiva.*

STORELVA runs from the town of Hønefoss to TYRIFJORDEN. The river is fairly deep in some areas and runs at a slow pace.

During autumn the TYRIFJORD trout run up to STORELVA for spawning and the average size trout caught in STORELVA in this period can be as large as 11lb.

The TYRIFJORDEN pike and bream do the same spawning run at spring time, and large pike are caught every year on trolling, spinning or deadbaiting.

**Access.**

Apart from the salmon fishing at Hellefossen in DRAMMENSELVA and trout fishing in the upper part of STORELVA north of Hønefoss (this part of the river is called RANDSELVA (32), all fishing is free.

Information about the salmon fishing can be obtained either from the Drammen Tourist Board or Hokksund Båt & Camping (telephone number 03 754242).

Licences are not expensive, compared to other Norwegian rivers (approximately 150 NOK a day), but limited. Special arrangements for tourists are available.

## AKERSVANNET AND BORREVANNET

**Location.**

AKERSVANNET (33) and BORREVANNET (34) are two medium sized, rich and shallow lakes, situated in the county of Vestfold, close to the Oslofjord.

AKERSVANNET is located in an agricultural area near the town of Tønsberg and gets covered with heavy reed growth and troubled with algae growth during late summer.

BORREVANNET, near the town of Horten, is not that overgrown or coloured, and bank access is a bit easier.

**Fish stocks.**

AKERSVANNET is stocked with bream, ide, rudd and dace, but mostly in smaller sizes. The predatory fish however, are both large and numerous. The lake holds large numbers of double figure pike, including the odd thirty pounder.

The zander have outnumbered the pike over the years and catches of 20-30 fish in an evening's session have been made. Big zander of 10-20lb are caught frequently.

AKERSVANNET also holds a good head of perch (to 3lb+) and eels.

In BORREVANNET, the ide and zander are extinct, but the lake provides excellent fishing for pike, perch and eel. As for the cyprinids, large numbers of smaller roach and bream and some medium sized rudd are present.

A smaller stock of tench is present, but very few are caught.

**Access.**

Fishing is free in both lakes and a boat is recommended. One should be aware of the algae problems in AKERSVANNET, as this makes the water poisonous, although it doesn't seem to be a problem with the fishing or fish.

# NUMEDALSLÅGEN RIVER

### Location.

The NUMEDALSLÅGEN (35) river is the second longest river in Norway, running down the Numedalen valley to the city of Larvik at the south east coast in the county of Vestfold, approximately 125km south of Oslo, along the E18. The water is clear, with very little weed growth, and changes character from rapid currents and waterfalls to slow stretches on its long journey to the sea.

### Fish stocks.

NUMEDALSLÅGEN is a famous salmon river and forty pounders are caught every season. Only the famous TANA river in the north of Norway produces more salmon a year. The lower stretches of NUMEDALSLÅGEN hold huge stocks of ide to 4-5lb, as well as pike, perch and eels.

In spring, the estuary provides good fishing for houting with fish to 6lb. Other species are sea trout, dace, bream and rudd.

### Access.

In NUMEDALSLÅGEN, a fishing licence must be purchased and for some of the more famous salmon pools, the number of licences are limited.

Fishing for houting in the estuary has, so far, been free.

Licences are sold by tackle dealers in Larvik, service stations, camp sites etc. Boats are available for hire.

## THE COURSE OF NORSJØ/SKIEN

### Location.

The course of Norsjø/Skien is one of the larger in Norway, including a number of large and medium sized lakes and rivers, all the way from the Hardangervidda plateau up in the mountains to the south east coast. It is, however, the lower parts which are of most interest to the coarse angler.

Lakes in the upper regions hold mostly smaller char and trout, and stocks are low due to problems from acid rain pollution (coming all the way from Britain).

The huge Hardangervidda plateau can, however, offer excellent wild trout and char fishing for anglers willing to take the trouble.

The river SKIENSELVA'S (36) outlet is close to the towns of Skien and Porsgrunn (in county Telemark) and runs from the large and deep lake NORSJØ (37). The two lakes BØRSESJØ (38) east of Skien and GUNNEKLEIVA (39) south of Porsgrunn are also worth mentioning in this context.

### Fish stocks.

NORSJØ holds predatory fish like pike, perch, wild brown trout and char to very good sizes. In May, as the smelt moves towards inlets for spawning, good catches of predatory fish can be expected.

NORSJØ has produced pike up to 40lb+, brown trout to 20lb and char to 10lb. There is a small stock of large crucian carp and finally, a lot of eels and small houting.

BØRSESJØ holds large quantities of good perch and rudd, but foremost an excellent head of large pike between 10 and 25lb+.

SKIENSELVA and GUNNEKLEIVA holds rudd to 2lb+, which, by Norwegian standards, must be ranked as very good. Bags of 60-70lb of rudd are recorded every year from GUNNEKLEIVA.

The area also holds large stocks of good quality perch and eels, in addition to pike, houting, salmon and sea trout.

### Access.

This area is situated approximately 150km south of Oslo along the E18.

In BØRSESJØ a boat is recommended, due to the heavy reed growth along most of the banks, and rowing boats are available for hire.

For the preservation of nesting water birds at BØRSESJØ, no angling is permitted prior to July 1st.

Fishing is free in most lakes and rivers, apart from the upper stretches of SKIENSELVA; a licence is needed for the salmon fishing (and can be obtained from tackle shops in Skien).

## ARENDAL AREA

### Location.

The town of Arendal is situated in the county of Aust-Agder on the south coast of Norway. The area holds a number of small and medium sized lakes.

### Fish stocks.

Although fish nowadays are present in a number of lakes in the southern part of Norway, Arendal provides the best tench fishing in Norway; almost every lake in the area is stocked with tench but the size and number varies.

In smaller lakes like SOLVERGVANN, DALETJERN and MOLANDSVANN, the tench average 1-2lb and larger specimens must be said to be very rare indeed. If the quarry is big bags of tench, these small lakes are consistent in performance and bags of 50+ tench are nothing extraordinary.

If specimen tench (by Norwegian standards) is the prey, the medium sized JOVANN, LANGSÆVANN and LONGUMVANN lakes are to be recommended. These lakes have produced a number of 5-6lb+ fish in recent years. The majority of the larger specimens (6lb) have all been male, which could indicate the maximum potential of female fish to be as large as 8 to 10lb.

Other species present in the Arendal region are pike, perch, eels, rudd, brown trout and American brook trout, but sizes and stocks must be classed as medium.

Fishing is best in the period May to August.

### Access.

Access to Arendal is straight forward - along the E18, either from OSLO or STAVANGER/KRISTIANSAND. There are a few very nice camp sites in this region, all with good facilities. Arendal town is one of the most popular summer resorts in Norway, but the lakes mentioned above are never crowded (to put it mildly).

*A big Norwegian perch in lovely condition.*

In lakes stocked with trout (like DALETJERN) a fishing licence is required, but in lakes with no trout, fishing is free. The banks of most lakes are quite overgrown so a bit of work has to be done in order to prepare a good swim. A good tip is to bring one of those inflatable boats.

*Jens Bursell with a huge bag of big tench.*

# Tour of Denmark

Denmark, like the rest of Scandinavia, offers the angler a wonderful opportunity to explore. It offers an amazing amount of untapped waters, just waiting for you to take off the cork. Let us make a tour of the country, stopping off at some beautiful and productive waters on the way.

We begin at the very north of **Jylland (Jutland)** at Hirtshals. To the west of Hirtshals runs the small Uggerby river near Bindslev, offering good sport in the late summer months with rainbow and brown trout to 6lb+, sea trout to over 16lb, and occasionally small salmon into double figures; also roach, perch, pike and eels.

Upstream, near Sindal, lies a lovely overgrown pool at Korsholt Plantage. This small 3½ acre lake holds pike to 20lb+, perch to 4lb+ and beautiful looking common carp to over 25lb. There are a number of other small pools close by, spreading over 55 acres.

Driving south on route 13, we cross the RyÅ (Å = river). This river holds sea, rainbow, and brown trout, double figure pike, perch over 2lb and bream up to 7lb.

We now drive south on the same road through Alborg until we reach Hobro. Just south of the town lies the Glenstrup lake holding pike into double figures, perch to 4lb+ and lake trout to 19lb+ (lake record - 17lb).

To the west of Hobro flow two rivers which enter the Hjarbæ fjord near Skals. The Simsted river to the north of Skals holds trout, tench, pike and good perch (mainly in autumn) to over 3lb. Good bream and perch to over 4lb can be caught in the Hjarbæk fjord itself (brackish water). The Skals river runs past a private lake near Hærup. This water holds carp to 37lb+ and numbers of 30lb+ pike, with some over 40lb. Carp have been netted in this water to over 45lb. Approach the landowner for permission if you wish to fish this special water.

North of Hærup, at Klejtrup, is a good lake holding trout to 5lb, perch over 3lb and a few large carp.

South of Hærup lake lies the Tjele long lake near Vinge. Primarily a boat fishery holding bream over 8lb, pike 20lb+, perch, tench and zander.

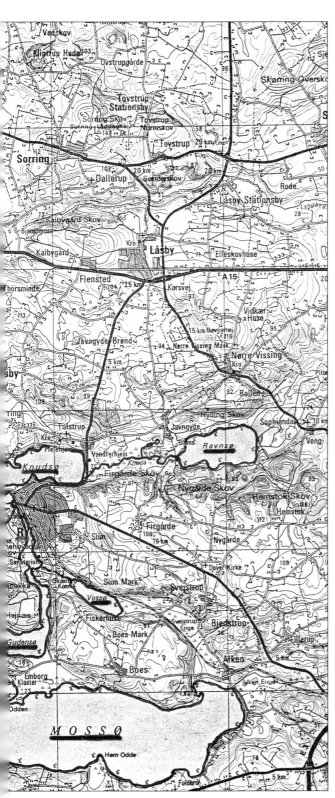

*Denmark, land of untapped
potential and prolific
coarse fishing.*

South west of Tjele lake, at Viborg, lie two large waters. Both the north and south lakes hold good fish, including pike to 25lb, bream 7lb+, zander to 9lb, carp to 30lb, rudd of 2lb+ and crucians to $3^1/_4$lb+.

On route 13, south of Viborg, lies the Ved lake holding bream, roach, pike, eels perch and a few large carp. Fishing is free for people in the Viborg Kommune (commune), but you may get permission whilst on holiday.

Hald lake lies a few km south of Ved, on the same road. This large water with depths of 10-30ft, holds pike over 20lb, perch over 21lb, trout to almost 10lb, and good bream, roach and eels.

20km south of Viborg near Ans, on the road to Arhus, lies the Tange lake. This large water holds pike to 20lb, zander to 13lb+, trout, big roach, tench (few), good perch (lake record $7^1/_2$lb!), and bream up to 11lb. Powan (whitefish) are also present (to over 4lb) in quite large numbers.

The Guden river runs through Tange lake and is one of the better known rivers amongst British anglers.

Downstream of Tange lake at Bjerringbø, good trout, roach, eels and bream to over 9lb are caught, including the odd salmon.

The Guden river runs throughout the Silkeborg lakes system and other good areas are at Langå, Resenbro, Vestbirk and Tørring. The upper reaches hold trout and large grayling; the middle and lower reaches hold sea trout to 20lb, bream to 9lb+, pike to 30lb, roach to 2lb+ and zander to 15lb+.

The Sninge lake (just before Resenbro) holds good pike up to 35lb.

When the Guden river reaches Silkeborg it runs through and past a series of lakes. The first is Silkeborg Long lake, which splits the town in two. This water holds pike to $39^1/_2$lb, perch 3lb+, zander 22lb+, bream to 11lb+, trout, roach and powan.

The river then runs into Brass lake, Almind lake, Thor lake, Borre lake, Jul lake, Birk lake, Guden lake and the huge Moss lake. All these waters hold good fish including pike over 20lb, zander to 17lb+, trout to 5lb+, crucians, perch and many roach and bream. Very large carp swim these waters, but they are very few in number.

The Salten lake, to the west of Moss lake, is strictly private. Directly east of Moss lake lies the big Skanderborg lake, holding large roach, zander, trout, eels, pike and large shoals of bream - although most of these are very small.

On the west side of Silkeborg town, at Lysbro, lies the Orn lake with pike to 22lb+, zander to 9lb, bream, roach, perch and trout.

To the south of Borre lake lies the Slåen lake. This beautiful water, surrounded on all sides by the Sønder woods, holds perch, bream, tench, roach and pike (up to 25lb).

Ravn lake lies to the west of Knud lake and the town of Ry. This large water holds bream, tench, burbot, crucians, powan, pike up to 35lb and many perch (some reaching 7lb!).

South of Silkeborg, at the town of Bryrup, are three lakes, Long lake, Kvind lake and Kul lake, all holding pike, bream, eel, perch and roach. Fishing in the Long lake is free but Kul lake is for the hotel guests only.

To the north of Skanderborg and just west of Hørning, is a small put-and-take trout fishery, with rainbows to almost 10lb.

Because of the incredible number of waters surrounding Silkeborg, it is an obvious choice for the all round angler to base himself. Tickets for most of the waters can be obtained at the majority of hotels, camp sites or club houses in the area, or from the Silkeborg Turistburea, Torvet 9, 8600 Silkeborg. Telephone 96 82 19 11.

For those who visit the area and wish to fish a small lake, there are a number of small pools (mose) just south of Ny Solberg, called Astrup Mose. These pools, 9 in all, feed the large Solberg lake and hold perch, eels, tench, small bream and pike to 25lb.

North of Solberg and west of Århus, runs the Arhus river, containing good fish, especially eels, with one specimen landed of over 6lb.

Near Feldballe (north west of Århus) lie two waters - the Long lake and Øje lake. Both of these hold big carp (many over 20lb), but you must obtain permission from the landowners before you fish.

The Stor river begins its travels west of Silkeborg, near the town of Ikast, and flows west to Nissum Fjord. It holds good rainbow trout, sea trout (best in late summer) to over $17\frac{1}{2}$lb, salmon to 35lb, pike to 20lb+, bream, roach, zander and perch. The best areas to fish are at Holstebro reservoir, at the junction of the Idam river (north of Kirby), and near Vemb.

North west of Holstebro and 9km west of Lemvig, lies a large water which nudges against the sand and winds of the North Sea. The Ferring lake contains pike, perch, roach and eels and fishing is free.

If we drive north west out of Holstebro to Vindrup, and then turn east on the road to Sevel, we enter an area with many lakes. The 7km long Flynder lake winds its way through woods and heath from Sevel to Rønberg. It holds perch up to $4\frac{1}{2}$lb, pike 20lb+, bream, roach, powan and large eels.

The large Stubbegård lake lies to the east of Sevel and holds pike to 20lb+, perch, eels, bream and roach. Fishing is free on the southern part of the lake. The northern area is surrounded by a number of smaller lakes and pools, and you should ask the landowners before fishing.

4km north east of Vindrup lies the Skan lake, containing bream, roach, good pike (20lb+), and rainbow trout to 11lb.

Holmgård lake is another free fishery with bream, roach and pike to over 20lb, but again, please contact the landowner first. The lake is situated at Kjeldsmark, 6km south of Vindrup.

We now travel south of Holstebro, to the town of Skjern. Here flows the river Skjern, which has produced sea trout up to $15\frac{1}{2}$lb, pike to 28lb, salmon over 22lb and good bream, perch, roach and grayling.

15km to the east of Skjern and just 1km south of Sønder Felding, is a good 29 acre trout lake. The water holds rainbows and brownies up to 13lb, field trout up to 5lb, pike into double figures, perch, eels, roach and carp.

Near the source of both the Skjern and Guden rivers, just south of Nørre Snede, the Skjern stream runs through four lakes. Rørbæk, the largest lake, holds pike (over 20lb), perch, bream, zander, roach, brown and rainbow trout. At the western end there is a camp site and restaurant. The stream then runs into Neder and Kul lakes, holding rainbows, grayling, pike, bream and eels.

Half a mile downstream the Skjern then runs into the 100 metre wide, 1km long Hastrup lake, holding the same species. The area surrounding the lake is a reserve, so fishing is only from one of the four punts owned by the club.

*Ulf Hausen with a fantastic 24¹/₂lb zander from Haralsted Lake.*

By driving south east on the road to Horsens, we cross a bridge on the upper reaches of the Guden river (mentioned in the Silkeborg section). 4km upstream of this bridge, near Uldam, lies the Uldam Kær. This is one lake, surrounded by twenty smaller pools, and five other pools a few hundred metres upstream! The fish in these lakes include zander into double figures, pike up to 23lb, bream 5lb+, roach, tench to 5lb+, trout, and a few grayling and burbot.

9km downstream of the bridge at Vestbirk lie three larger lakes, holding the same species; there is a lakeside camp site.

South of Vestbirk and on the western edge of Horsens town, lies the 3km long Bygholm lake, holding good eels, perch, roach, sea trout and pike into the upper twenties.

We now drive on the E3 road south to Vejle. 10km to the west of town and 2km south of Jelling lies another 'boat only' fishery called Fårup lake. This large, 2km long, 1km wide lake holds pike up to 37¹/₂lb, good perch, with some reaching 4lb+, trout to 13lb+ and decent bream.

Just 4km to the south west of Fårup lies the Englesholm lake near Nørup. This water is about half the size of Fårup and contains 20lb+ pike, perch to 2lb+, bream, crucians, zander and a small head of carp to 20lb+.

*Erik Green with a wonderful 20$^1/_4$lb trout from Bornholm.*

*Tony with part of a huge haul of crucian carp from a lake near Copenhagen. Many of the fish are over 4lb!*

*Jens Bursell with part of a huge haul of big bream from the Simested River on Jutland.*

10km south of Engelsholm, near the village of Spjarup, are three small lakes covering 2½ acres, holding rainbows up to 11lb, brownies to 6½lb and carp into upper doubles.

Close to here is another small water called Hvilested Lystfisker lake, with brownies up to 7lb, rainbows up to 15lb and small carp and field trout.

The 176 road heads south east through Egtved to Vester Nebel. This is quite a good place to base yourself with one ticket covering the Harte-Dons lakes and streams in the area. The north lake, called Norre lake, holds carp up to 30lb+ (low stock per acre), pike to upper twenties, bream, tench, etc. Norre lake then runs into Sønder lake which stretches for 2km before bending back on itself into a 1km long backwater. This water holds similar fish to the north lake, although, to my knowledge, no carp have yet been taken - but I very much doubt that it doesn't hold carp!

A stream runs out of Sønder lake and enters the 1½km long Stellerup lake, just 2km downstream. This lake is a good predator water, with pike to over 33lb, perch to 3¼lb and zander into double figures.

Stellerup then runs into the long, narrow Påby lake.

We now travel west on the E66 towards Esbjerg, which may be the first port of call for many British anglers. 15km after Grimstrup and 20km before Esbjerg, we turn right on the 11 road towards Varde for 9km, then turn left to Vester Nebel (a different town to the previously mentioned Vester Nebel!). Here lie four small lakes and one larger lake, covering approximately 11 acres in all. They contain carp to 27lb, tench to 4lb+, pike to 15lb+, bream to 5lb, trout to 7lb, perch, and good eels to 4½lb.

The river Varde runs through the town of Varde and this river holds good pike, perch, roach and rainbows, with a few grayling and occasional salmon. It is best known for its sea trout during the autumn, with specimens to 13lb+.

Up river, 7km east of Varde is a 3½km long, beautiful lake holding big pike to 30lb, bream to 13lb, trout to 11lb and carp of unknown potential.

Further downstream still, at the town of Grindsted, the river Grindsted tributary runs through the 1½km long Eng lake. This water contains 20lb+ pike, tench, roach and large shoals of bream.

If we take the 181 and 431 roads west of Varde, we come to Oksbol. To the north west of town lies the Præste lake, containing good bream and tench, pike to 23lb, perch to 2½lb and rainbows over 6½lb.

We now drive south of Esbjerg on the 11 road and cross the Kong river at Gredstedbro, which holds sea trout to 17lb, and then on to Ribe. Here, the river Ribe runs through the town and contains pike, perch, bream, roach - and a chance to latch onto a sea trout of over 22lb!

Heading east now from Ribe, on the 437 road, through Rødding, we come to Jels. To the north of town lie three lakes in tandem. The most northerly lake, called Overlake, is a bird reserve but the larger middle and southerly (Neder) lakes offer good fishing. The lakes' depths average around 5-15ft with some areas over 30ft. Both waters contain good pike up to low thirties, zander, perch, bream, trout and roach. Big carp swim these waters, but they are few in number.

At the town of Haderslev is a very large, 5km long lake, called Haderslev Dam. It contains large stretches of reed beds and is best tackled from a boat. It is good, mixed fishing, with bream, perch (2½lb), pike (20lb+), zander (9lb), trout

(8lb+) and good crucians and roach. Large carp swim in this lake, but again, few in number per acre.

A lovely looking water, called Stevning Dam, lies to the east of here, just over the E3 motorway on the eastern edge of Hammelev town. A good, mixed fishery, with pike, roach and bream, and with a better chance of contacting carp. Parts of the south wood and backwater are private.

The Pamhule lake, just south of Haderslev Dam, near Marstrup, holds good fish - roach and rudd over 3lb and common carp over 33lb, but it is private and you must obtain permission first.

We now drive south west on the 435 to Tønder, near the West German border. To the south of town the Vid river flows through a lovely area of lakes and backwaters and contains good pike, zander, bream, tench, roach, eels and trout.

We travel east along the border, through Grasten (the castle lake holds big carp but is strictly private!) and Sonderborg, then on to the island of Als. Just past Almsted, on route 8, are two lakes holding pike, carp and tench, but you must contact the Sportfishing administration on 74 43 31 96 for permission to fish.

The Kelling Nor, near Ketting, is another water controlled by this same club and is a boat fishery with many species, including perch to 5lb+.

You should have no problem obtaining permission for the $2^1/_2$km long lake at Nordborg - just go to the Nordals tourist office in Nordborg! This lake holds zander to 6lb+, pike to 20lb, good roach and many (mainly small) bream. It also holds some large carp but, again, these are very few per acre.

Well, that's Jutland over with! I hope I'm not boring you, but if it's information you need for your trip - here it is!

We now drive over the bridge at Middlefart (that's a pleasant name for a town isn't it?), or take the ferry from Als, to the large island of **Fyn (Funen).** This island offers primarily coastal fishing for sea trout (and very good ones at that, especially around Svendborg and Langeland), but it does offer a few good day ticket waters.

North east of Odense on the 303, and south of the town of Marud, is a $1^1/_4$km long lake. The Lange lake holds good perch to 3lb, with some over 4lb, big pike to upper twenties, many bream and roach, zander to 7lb and a few decent tench.

The Odense river, especially at Munkemose, holds a good mixture of fish with pike, zander, bream, ide, roach, perch, trout and the odd salmon.

The lakes near the castle in Nyborg provide good coarse fishing for tench up to 5lb, pike, bream, crucians and a few large carp.

The Hokenhavn Fjord to the south of town has produced some large perch and ide.

A number of lakes on Fyn hold pike and carp over 30lb, but these are all strictly private and obtaining permission from the landowners is difficult. The small lake and moat surrounding the Broholm castle holds tench to 7lb+ and rudd to 3lb+; the water is owned by an Englishman, who sometimes gives permission to holiday anglers.

A ferry crosses the short stretch of sea (ships every hour, and a tunnel is being built) to Korsor on **Sjæland.**

Driving east on the E66 motorway, we turn off at Søro. Here lie two waters, the Pederborg and Søro lakes; both hold big fish with pike to 20lb+, zander to 17lb,

*A sample of the carp fishing Denmark can provide is shown in these pictures of Johnny Jensen and Tony Davies-Patrick.*

perch over 3lb and bream, roach, tench and lake trout.

Further south on the 157 road, near Eskilstrup, is the large Tystrup lake. This 7km long, 2km wide water, with depths from 4-16 metres, offers very good fishing, with zander to 22lb+, pike 35lb+, perch and powan to over 3lb, roach over 2lb, tench, and bream to 6lb+. The smaller Bavelse lake connects to the southern end of Tystrup lake and provides fishing of the same calibre.

8km south of Bavelse is a small lake containing large perch, pike to 22lb, bream and small carp.

North of Slagelse, on route 22, and 7km east of Gørlev lies the huge, circular, Tiss lake. This water slopes gradually from 5ft to 36ft in depth, and is better fished from a boat. It contains perch to 4lb+, zander to 17lb and pike to over 40lb!

We now drive east of Slagelse on the motorway, past Søro, and turn off at Ringsted towards Merløse. 5km north of Ringsted, we cross the western edge of the large and long Haraldsted lake. This wonderful water, with average depths of 3-15ft, holds pike over 33lb, perch up to $4\frac{1}{2}$lb and good bream, tench and roach; but it is the zander which grow to really big weights here, with the largest recorded weighing a fantastic $24\frac{1}{4}$lb!!

Just to the west of Haraldsted is the equally large Gyrstinge lake. This water holds pike into upper twenties, zander to upper doubles and many bream and roach. Many zander lie along the steep shelf which edges along the north bank.

The Sus/Ringsted rivers near Ringsted, hold various species, including bream over 6lb and big ide to 5lb.

A good, day ticket (25 Kroner), fishery is the Lammefjords canal north of Holbæk, near Hagested; here run two streams. The northern canal contains tench to $5\frac{1}{2}$lb, carp up to 10lb, bream, roach, and pike to upper doubles. The canals are heavily populated with wildies and offer quite hectic sport at times. The southern canal contains many commons (to 20lb), but fewer wildies than the northern canal, and roach to 2lb, ide to 4lb+, sea and rainbow trout to 4lb and many big rudd (2lb+) shoals.

We now travel east from Holbæk on the E66 motorway and turn off just before København (Copenhagen) at the Alberlstund/Vallensbæk junction. The Vallensbæk lake lies on the southern side of the motorway and the Tueholm lake · on the northern side; a short canal joins both waters and therefore they contain the same fish.

The Vallensbæk lake is quite an open water, with one small island.

The Tueholm lake is much more attractive, with numerous islands, bays and reed beds.

These lakes contain mirror carp to 35lb, grass carp to 20lb, crucians to $4\frac{1}{2}$lb, tench to $5\frac{1}{2}$lb, good eels and double figure pike.

Close by, on the northern edge of Tåstrup, lies the Hakke pool and Dybendal lake. The Dybendal contains pike, tench, crucians and grass carp. The Hakke mosen (pool) holds bream to 5lb, pike over 20lb, tench, and the odd zander.

The Utterslev lakes in the centre of the city in the Utterslev/Brønshoj sectors, contain various species, including tench to 7lb and crucians over $3\frac{1}{2}$lb.

On the outer areas of København, near Kongenslyngby, lie two large waters - the Bagværd lake and the smaller Lyngby lake. They both contain pike up to 35lb, zander into double figures (18lb), perch to $2\frac{1}{2}$lb, bream, and carp into double figures. Some larger carp are present, but they are few in numbers. Bagsværd is a comparatively shallow water with average depths of 3-6ft. The Lyngby lake runs into the huge Fure lake near Virum. This large, and windswept expanse of water, with depths of 5-27ft, provides very good sport for the predator angler, with pike reaching 20lb+, many double figure zander, with the chance of 20lb+ fish, and good perch to 3½lb. It also holds roach, bream, crucians, tench and burbot.

At the north east corner at Fiskebæk, the Fure lake joins the Farum lake. This lovely looking water, skirted by woods along the southern shoreline, and nudged by Farum town to the north, provides excellent sport, with pike to upper twenties, perch to 4lb+, zander to 15lb, burbot to 6½lb, roach, tench and many bream.

Sjæl lake to the north of Fure lake, near Ravnsnæs, contains good perch to 5lb+ and pike to 20lb+.

The beautiful looking Donse Dam (lake), 3½km north west of Sjæl lake and surrounded by woods, is a good pike water with many double figure pike up to 28lb and nice perch and crucians.

East of Sjæl lake, near Hørsholm, is the small Spring Dam. This water holds very good crucians, with some reaching over 4lb.

Further north, at Fredensborg, is the massive lake, (or should I say inland sea?!) called Esrum lake. This holds many 20lb+ pike, with some to upper thirties, roach to 3lb, good perch, large shoals of bream (3-7lb) and a few tench.

The even bigger Arre lake to the east, at Annisse, (and this **is** an inland sea!) offers free fishing for zander, bream, pike, perch and tench. Although the water has lost its edge over recent years, it still offers the chance of upper double figure zander, the best areas being around Lille Lyngby and Kregme at the southern end.

The Gurre lake, to the north east of Esrum, between Tikøb and Gurre, is a lovely looking water with vast reed beds and enclosed in a large wood. This 294 acre lake contains perch over 3½lb, good pike, bream, roach and tench.

Two good trout waters lie to the north east of Gurre in the Teglstrup woods south of Hellebæk. Both the Kare and Sort lakes hold rainbows to 5lb, but also contain pike over 20lb (with some up to 30lb), perch and golden tench.

We now travel south of København on the east coast road to Kastrup. The Karlstrup lake is a superb trout water with specimens up to 15lb! Carrying on south through Kage we cross the Tryggevælde river just before Strøby Egede. This river is a classic perch stream, with many big fish moving upstream from the brackish water to Stroby and Hårlev during spring. Specimens are in the 2-4lb class; other fish include bream, carp, ide, pike and sea trout.

Route 209 takes us south again through Hårlev and Fakse, until we see a large inlet to the left, just after Vindbyholt village. The Præste Fjord is quite a special place. In spring, the double figure sea trout enter the fjord and in both spring and autumn hundreds of brackish water perch between 2-5lb and pike to 20lb+ enter into this large inlet of the sea. There are three camp sites around the fjord's coastline.

Most of the fjords and coastal inlets in this area, and on Lolland island to the south, provide good fishing for perch, but Præsto is one of the best for those who have dreamed of a monster 'sergeant' since their early schoolboy days!

Travelling south from Præsto, on the E4, we cross the two bridges to Lolland and drive on until we reach Maribo. The Norre lake (to the north of town), contains pike and carp into double figures, bream to 5lb+, tench to 6lb+ and perch to 3lb.

The huge and wonderful Sønder lake to the south, is really three lakes in one, with many islands, bays, channels and large reed beds. The western section covers about 1200 acres, the middle section about 740 acres and the long, eastern arm about 700 acres. The water is comparatively little fished, due mainly to soft marshland along most of its shoreline. If you can manage to bring an inflatable, or borrow a boat (outboards are banned), you can try to untap the unknown potential of this lake. It holds large carp, pike, bream, perch and roach.

South east of Sønder lake and just west of Store Musse and Herritslev are a number of small pools and lakes, covering approximately 37 acres, called the Karsgårds Sportfiskeri, which provide good sport for trout, perch to 3lb+, tench to 5lb+ and bream.

West from Herritslev (on route 297 and then south on the E4 to Rødbyhavn) are the Hirbo lakes, providing good mixed fishing for pike, bream, crucians (2lb+), perch and both tench and eels to $4\frac{1}{2}$lb.

We now travel on the last leg of our Danish tour, to Nakskov, before taking the ferry to Bornholm. On the north western edge of town, near Hellenæs and Sandvadet, are a group of small lakes with the largest at just under 20 acres, which hold pike, carp, bream and roach.

To the south of town lies the Indre Fjord near Lienlund. This brackish water inlet from the sea holds big pike, bream, eels, roach (to $2\frac{1}{2}$lb), tench and big perch ($2\frac{3}{4}$lb), especially during the spring months.

**Bornholm island**, situated in the East sea, off the southern Sweden coast, is not usually thought of by visitors to Denmark, but this Danish island offers good opportunities to get amongst some big fish. Regular ferries run from København in Denmark (7 hours) and Ysted in Sweden ($2\frac{1}{2}$ hours). Superb sea trout fishing with specimens up to 20lb+ can be caught all along the coastline, but one special place is the Rønne town harbour area which has produced a number of pike over 20lb, with some reaching over 30lb. The harbour also holds rainbow trout over $8\frac{1}{2}$lb, perch to 2lb+ and ide up to $6\frac{1}{2}$lb. What other town ocean harbour holds fish like this? - all you get off Bristol harbour is oil slicks!

On the northern tip of the island, just west of Sanvig town, is one major lake and three smaller pools. The larger water, called Hammer lake, is about 650 metres long and 150 metres wide. It holds double figure pike, roach over 2lb, perch 3lb+, crucians 2lb+, trout to 5lb and offers very good tench fishing with some specimens to almost 9lb.

A put-and-take trout fishery (called Stembrud lakes) lies close to Neksø on the south east coast. These small pools, as well as having 3,000 trout chucked into them annually, hold zander to 10lb+, crucians 2lb+ and small perch.

The Svinemose is a picturesque lake with three islands, in the centre of Almindingen forest, nestling between two hills. It contains tench, perch, roach and pike to 28lb.

The Krashavemose, a narrow, 900 metre long lake, to the north east of Klemensker, also holds large pike, with some over 30lb, tench to $6\frac{1}{2}$lb, crucians, and thousands of small roach and perch to feed those big pike!

*Leon Hoogendijk with a superb 33½lb mirror from Sarrebourg.*

# Big Carp in The East of France

For the most fanatical carp anglers, fishing every weekend during the season isn't enough; they want to put as much time as possible into their hobby and are fishing for big carp even during their holidays.

Many of them come to France every year, searching for a second lake Cassien, which they will probably not find. They don't realise that even in France, Lake Cassien is a very exceptional 'lac'. I don't say that lakes with a population of very big carp comparable to those of St. Cassien don't exist in France, but there are few of them and France is a very big country. True, other lakes and rivers in France have produced huge fish in excess of 50 or 60 pounds, but not in the same number as from St. Cassien. Don't think that every water here is packed with big carp, because they aren't. In fact, in some parts of the country, carp fishing is very hard indeed.

Since 1986 I've been fishing in France regularly and since November, 1987 I've lived in Chalon sur Saône, a small town between Dijon and Lyon, in the Province Saône et Loire, which is possibly one of the best provinces for carp fishing in France. There are some good rivers, big lakes and hundreds of gravel pits, all containing big carp from between 30lb up to 60lb+, and many of these waters are not being fished seriously for carp.

I'm lucky to have some good (not easy) waters not far from my home. Many Dutch and English people spend their holidays in my region every year, fishing for big carp. Most of them return home disappointed after having blanked or had poor results. In many cases this is because they have fished in the wrong way. The most common faults they make are overbaiting swims and/or not being prepared to move swims.

Almost all the waters in my region are extremely rich in natural food, which is, of course, the main reason for producing big fish, and a growth rate of 3 or 4 pounds a year is not unusual. These natural riches of food consist of crayfish, freshwater mussels and all kinds of insects and their larva. The carp in these waters are not hungry, so why should you put in 30, 40, or 50 pounds of particles in a swim? In most lakes I have had far better results when baiting with only a handful of particles, or 20 boilies per fishing rod! Another problem of heavy prebaiting is that it attracts many small carp and it's impossible to realise the potential of a 'baiting pyramid' in one or two weeks if you are fishing the swim right from the start.

In many of the lakes and gravel pits here, the carp feed on crayfish in the shallow margins during the night but, unfortunately, night fishing is not allowed here. During daylight hours the carp are further away from the banks in the deeper water, but are not very active. This doesn't mean that you can't catch them; the carp are often in a group in a holding area and if you find them and put just a few baits in, then the carp are quite willing to take these. If you overbait the swim you can forget about having any action (remember, the carp are not active at this time).

In the bigger lakes (100 acres+), the carp are moving about a lot so you have to move with them; observation is the key factor. It is quite rare to find a swim that produces big fish for longer than two days. In most cases, if you find the fish and you fish correctly, then you can catch some big carp in the first 24 hours; after this you'll start catching small ones and this indicates when it's time to move.

*Leon with a low Twenty from a 4,000 acre lake.*

For big carp, it isn't necessary to fish only the huge lakes (barrages). There are also many smaller lakes in my region (gravel pits from 20-80 acres), which hold very big carp. You are more likely to succeed on these 'small' lakes during your holidays because the location of fish is much easier.

## BAIT

The ideal size of your boilies is between $^3/_4$ and $1^1/_2$ inches in diameter and they should be rock hard to resist the attacks of crayfish and the small American catfish. Flavours like strawberry, Scopex or Tutti-Frutti are working instantly (in lakes). Use a simple mix, HP or HNV baits are a waste of time and money. I'm using ingredients like semolina, maize meal, soya meal, etc., and a small amount of casein and calcium caseinate to improve the structure of my baits. With $1^1/_2$ inch boilies I haven't caught a carp under 18lb yet!

I prefer short hairs and stiff hooklinks (30.00mm mono) because I have found that longer hairs and/or soft hooklinks will often tangle, due to the crayfish and small catfish which play with the baits for many hours until the carp arrive. Use simple rigs and fish with tight lines if you are not fishing in the margins.

If the bottom of the lake is hard and clean, which is often the case in most lakes here, and you are not fishing over a carpet of baits, then bottom baits will give better results than pop-ups.

## RIVERS

It is not only the lakes and 'barrages' that produce big fish, but also many rivers hold very large carp. The biggest (rod caught) carp in Europe came from a French river ($81^1/_2$lb). This fish was caught by M. Rouviere from Montereau and measured 39" in length, with a 47" girth.

Whilst in most lakes 90% of the fish are mirror and leather carp, in most rivers 90% are common carp, and although boilies work instantly in the lakes, in the rivers this isn't the case.

In spring 1988, I was fishing a famous catfish river (Seille), 20 miles from my home. The river does hold carp but nobody fishes for them. Fishing with maize (corn), I soon found a producing swim and I decided to do a baiting campaign with boilies. During one week I put loads of boilies into the swim every day; after this I fished with boilies, along with maize, and had many runs on the maize, catching carp up to about 25lb, but nothing on the boilies. Switching rods didn't make any difference. Friends of mine had exactly the same experience on other rivers. I think I have an explanation of the phenomenon but I am not 100% sure of my theory, so I will not bother you with it. However, maize is the bait for river carp.

In rivers you don't have to be afraid of overbaiting your swim - in the current (sometimes very strong), the carp are moving and feeding all the time. I usually put about 10-15lb of particles in my swim, and by doing this I can expect action the whole day long. Don't worry that you can't fish at night because if you do, you will see that 90% of the runs will come during daylight hours - so you're better off having a good sleep and saving your energy for the next day.

The problem in rivers is that although there are very big carp, there are also loads of small carp (2-10lb), but fishing with 4 or 5 grains of maize on a hair, I rarely caught carp under 10lb. I use the same rig as I use in the lakes.

## WHERE TO FISH:

The location of carp isn't as easy as it is in the lakes and if the fish are showing themselves, it often doesn't indicate a feeding area, but the route in which the carp are moving from one point to another. For example in the Saône, a very large river that holds hundreds-thousands of carp (up to 60lb+), the fish often show themselves in the deeper channel of the river, while most people have their best results fishing at very close range. In the smaller, but more beautiful, rivers like the Seille, fishing is more difficult because these rivers hold fewer carp, but of a better average size, so some knowledge of these rivers is necessary to succeed.

The diagram shows a typical feeding area in a small river.

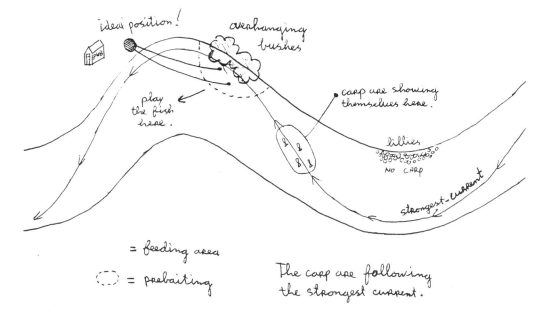

idea position!

overhanging bushes

play the fish here.

carp are showing themselves here.

lillies

NO CARP

strongest-current

= feeding area

= prebaiting

The carp are following the strongest current.

## CONCLUSION:

If you decide to spend your holidays carp fishing in the East of France, you should realise that you don't have any guarantee of catching big fish. There are, perhaps, one or two short periods in a year when you can really score heavily in a water, so if you come only one or two weeks in a year you'll probably miss those periods and will have to work hard for your catches. Believe me, even a virgin water can be very hard to fish, but for totally different reasons than a pressured water.

As you can see, La Saône et Loire is full of interesting waters; many of them are still unfished and what is more exciting than catching a big carp in a water and swim that you have discovered for yourself - that's **real** carp fishing!

# Night Fishing in the East of France

For those of you who want to fish for carp at night legally in France, there is one exceptional possibility. On the east side of Chalon sure Saône, there is a 60 acre lake called Le Lac de la Zup, and it's the only lake in France (at the time of writing), where night fishing is allowed.

The lake is about 20 years old and has depths of over 30 feet in the centre; the bottom is a mixture of sand and clay and is reasonably hard and clean. The lake has produced carp to 40lb and was stocked with carp up to 50lb in the spring of 1989. There is also a good head of grass carp ('amour-blanc') up to about 25lb. The growth rate of these grass carp is more than 5lb per year and in 1990 we expect thirties!

*Paul Breedveld with a beautiful Zup lake 30lb+ mirror.*

The lake is not an easy water, but with a little luck you should be able to hook one or two big carp if you fish correctly for, let's say, a week. During the night the carp often feed in the shallow margins and can be caught at depths between 3 and 6 feet. Again, don't overbait the swim and be ready to move every 2 or 3 days. The only swims where you can put more bait in and expect action for the whole week are the Island pitches (left and right), which are holding and feeding areas at the same time. These swims produce carp during daylight hours, especially during the morning in sunny weather.

The lake was discovered by some Dutch anglers in 1985. Most of them were overbaiting their swims and had poor results, while I caught big carp on every trip, baiting up with only 10-15 boilies per fishing rod! There is still no pressure on the lake, although during the last two years there have been some locals fishing for carp on a regular basis. Licences can be bought at any tackle shop.

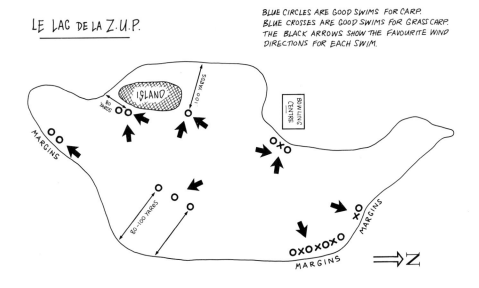

LE LAC DE LA Z.U.P.

BLUE CIRCLES ARE GOOD SWIMS FOR CARP.
BLUE CROSSES ARE GOOD SWIMS FOR GRASS CARP.
THE BLACK ARROWS SHOW THE FAVOURITE WIND
DIRECTIONS FOR EACH SWIM.

The first time that I fished Zup lake, back in 1986, with my good friend Paul Breedveld, we both thought that we had discovered a second lake Cassien. Little was known about the lake but the locals told us stories about monster carp that they had lost.

On our first day on the lake we saw enormous carp jumping out of the water at 100 yards plus, which boosted our already strong confidence and optimism. The first three fish we caught were good twenties. We thought they were small ones and the big ones had yet to come - but we were wrong and only caught some low doubles and small grass carp during the week.

We never thought to visit the lake again until a message arrived from our French friend, Dominique Darcy, who had caught some big carp up to 40lb in October, so we planned a session for the next spring.

*Leon with a Zup biggie.*

In early May, Paul and I were back for a one week session. The first four days and nights we fished in pouring rain without having any action, but when the rain stopped we had our revenge and both took some upper twenties, topped by an immaculate 30lb+ leather for Paul!

Two weeks later we had yet another message from Dominique; in the week after our visit he had taken 18 carp, 15 of which were between 26 and 40lb!

I returned again a few times that year and caught big carp, although the monsters escaped me time after time. By the end of the year, quite a few carp were caught more than once and led us to believe that the lake only held a small population of big carp. Almost all of those carp were mirrors and leathers.

I was very surprised when, in 1988, the lake suddenly produced quite a number of 20lb+ commons, topped by a fish of 35lb! The small grass carp were coming out as twenties by now!

In 1987, both Dominique Darcy and my friend Erwin Vlat observed a carp which they both estimated at 55lb, while André van der Schaft observed a 40lb+ common in the same year.

In 1989, the lake was stocked with some more twenty pounders, including a specimen of 50lb!

Those three fish are the biggest carp I know of in this lake, but they have yet to be caught. My friend Leo Westdorp probably hooked such a fish in September, 1986 while fishing at close range with peanuts on light glass rods. The fish simply emptied his spool! The same thing happened to Dominique Darcy one year later; this time on a heavy rod and 12lb line!

# French Carp Waters

Most carp anglers who like to spend their fishing holidays in France, are not willing to search for a suitable big carp water. They simply don't have the time for it, or don't like the risk which goes along with pioneering. Others don't care about the size of the carp, all they want is a bend in their rod, to do some fun fishing, or to visit a typical holiday water with their wife and children.

For all those people, I've made a selection of 28 French waters. The limited information I give about these waters is verified. For obvious reasons, no small waters are mentioned in the list.

1. **Les etanges de Biscarosse.** Complex of two very big, shallow lakes, 30 miles south of Bordeaux and only a few miles from the Atlantic ocean. **L'Etang de Parentis** is reputed to hold monster carp, but location of fish is difficult and will take at least several days (if not a week!). Both very hard lakes and only recommended for those who are finished at Cassien!

2. **Calais** (north of France). **Le canal de Guines** and <u>**Le canal de Calais.**</u> Both canals hold many small and medium sized carp - easy waters.

3. **St. Cassien.** In 1989 the lake again produced some 'unknown' monsters, so the mystery is still alive! (Remember, twenties become thirties, thirties become forties, and...).

4. **Chalain** (near Lons le Saunier/Jura). a 500 acre lake. Typical holiday water to visit with the whole family. Produced a forty pound carp to a match angler in 1989! Beautiful surroundings.

5. **Reservoir de Chazilly** (near Neaune/Bourgogne). Beautiful surroundings. Superb 'lac de barrage' holding carp of all sizes; big shallow plateaus in the southern part of the lake with a lot of vegetation.

6. <u>**St. Croix**</u> (near Cassien). Huge 'lac de barrage', holding monster carp (several carp between 50 and 80 pounds reported). The location of the carp is difficult because of the enormous size of the lake (5,500 acres). However, if you find the fish you can expect a lot of action. Didier Cottin and his friends caught some good carp here in 1989.

7. **Lac d'Aiguebelette** (near Chambery, eastern France). A beautiful 600 acre lake holding a large number of 30lb+ carp, up to over 50lb - a semi-difficult water.

8. **Jugon les lacs** (near St. Malo, north west France). Two lakes of 200 and 450 acres. Not easy, but both lakes have produced numbers of 40lb+ carp over the last few years.

9. **St. Geniez d'Olt** (Aveyron). Very popular carp lake, holding loads of small common and mirror carp (5-15lb) with some bigger fish (some commons reaching 40lb+). Access is difficult in places, due to steep wooded cliffs: a boat (available for hire) can be an advantage. Ideal for fun fishing - up to 30 carp a day is not unusual here, but remember, like all lakes, it does have its slow periods occasionally!

10. **La Loire** (from Nantes via Tours and Orleans to Nevers). A Superb, shallow river with most parts holding lots of common carp to all sizes.

Recommended for family holidays is **Le Loire a Montjean** near Angers in the west of France.

11. **Le lac de Madine** (near Metz). 2,700 acres; easy carp water (fish of all sizes), in beautiful surroundings.

12. **Reservoirs de la Marne** (near Langres). 4 lakes from 250 to 700 acres. Recommended for carp is **La Retenue de Charmes** which holds many carp of good sizes.

13. **Lac de Nantua** (near Geneve). 400 acre lake near the Alps, holding good stocks of carp of all sizes.

*The famous Lake Cassien in the South of France.*

124

*The Castelnau Lake near St. Geniez d'Olt.*

*Leon with a twenty pound grass carp from Zup Lake.*
*Below: Leon cradles a lovely 34lb leather carp.*

14. **Barrage de Pannecieres-Chaumard** (near Autun, east-central France). Beautiful 1,300 acre lake with an, as yet, unknown potential. Carp to over 40lb were caught by some match anglers in 1989. A very rich water.

15. **Lac de Pareloup** (near Rodez, south of France). Huge lake renowned for its carp population; carp to over 40lb.

16. **Les etanges du pays de Sarrebourg** (near Strasburg, north east France). Complex of reservoirs (over 5,000 acres in all). A very popular carp complex, holding some very big carp! ** see notes.

17. **Le lac de Pont** (Semur en Auxois, near Dijon). Lake of 250 acres, rich in vegetation and natural food; carp of all sizes.

18. **Lac de Rabodanges** (near Cean, north west France). Another shallow, 250 acre lake. No pressure and many carp up to about 40lb.

19. **Salagou** (near Beziers, south of France). 1,800 acres; one of Didier Cottin's favourite lakes. Holds carp to well over 50lb. Location of fish can take several days. (Very strong winds sometimes whip up on this lake and the carp move with it. In some areas you can encounter problems similar to Cassien, namely, tree stumps etc., so it is advisable to use tactics and rigs to overcome this: Tony).

20. **Saône** (eastern France). Large river holding loads of common carp. 40lb+ commons are caught every year! The best parts for carp are between Chalon sur Saône and Lyon. The river also holds many enormous catfish to over 200lb! (158$\frac{1}{2}$lb catfish landed during 1990).

21. **Seille** (in the Saône valley). Beautiful, small river holding both mirrors and commons to over 40lb. Best parts are La Truchére, Cuisery and Louhans. Also catfish to about 120lb!

22. **Seine.** Big river holding big fish! Many commons of all sizes. Best parts, **Monterau** for very big carp (European record caught here, at 81$\frac{1}{2}$lb), and **Andelys** for a lot of action with mainly medium sized carp. 63lb common (biggest in French history) caught on sweetcorn in 1990.

23. **Les Settons** (near barrage de Rannecieres). Big, shallow lake. Typical holiday water with loads of small carp - up to 30 a day possible.

24. **Barrage de la Sorme** (near Autun and Le Creusot). Big 'lac de barrage' with an, as yet, unknown potential. In 1987 and 1988 **three** forty pound carp were caught on **live baits!!** Stocked with mirror carp many years ago, but nobody is fishing for them. Large shoals of big carp were observed by some friends of mine in July, 1987.

25. **Vasiviere** (near Limoges, central France). A 2,900 acre carp lake, which is very popular and holds many carp over 25lb.

26. **Lac de Vezins** (near Avranches, north west France). A beautiful, river-like 'lac de barrage' holding loads of carp of all sizes.

27. **Villeneuve la Raho** (near Perpignan, extreme south of France). 400 acre lake, a few miles from the Mediterranean sea. A nice holiday water holding loads of carp.

28. **Lac de Vouglans** (near Lons le Saunier and Jura). A superb 4,000 acre lake in beautiful surroundings. Loads of carp between 10 and 25lb in the northern part of the lake. Rumours about monster carp from the larger, southern part of the lake.

** In the list of French carp waters I've mentioned 'Les Etangs de Sarrebourg' (N/E). I've been there with my friend Leo Westdorp this year (we'll return next year) and I am convinced that it's the future French carp paradise. Here are some more details:

Total of six lakes from 500 to 2500 acres and over 100 years old. All lakes are shallow, between 6 and 12 feet, with roots and enormous weedbeds everywhere and extremely rich in natural food (snails, mussels, crayfish, bloodworm etc). All lakes contain large numbers of big, and very big, carp to over 50lb.

The biggest carp from the lakes was a 77lb mirror caught in the nets by a professional fisherman from the lake 'Etang du Stock' (the biggest lake), stuffed and exposed at Nancy. Also reports of a 63.8lb mirror and a 55lb leather caught by carp anglers in 1990.

All fish are pure Galicians and are the most beautiful and nicely coloured I have ever seen.

Most popular lakes: Gondrexange and Le Petit Etang (1400 and 400 acres).

The biggest handicap, access is very difficult so it is necessary to walk long distances with all your gear. Not recommended for lazy anglers!

*Geoff Shaw returns a beautifully scaled French mirror carp.*

A beautiful atmospheric shot of Lake Vouglans.
Leon Hoogendijk holds a superb, heavily scaled French mirror.

*Sunset over Sarrebourg.*

*Above. A big, hard fighting French common from Sarrebourg for Leon.*

*Left. the river Cher at Thesée holds good barbel and zander.*

French star Didier Cottin with terrific St.Cassien carp of 43$\frac{1}{2}$lb and 57lb.

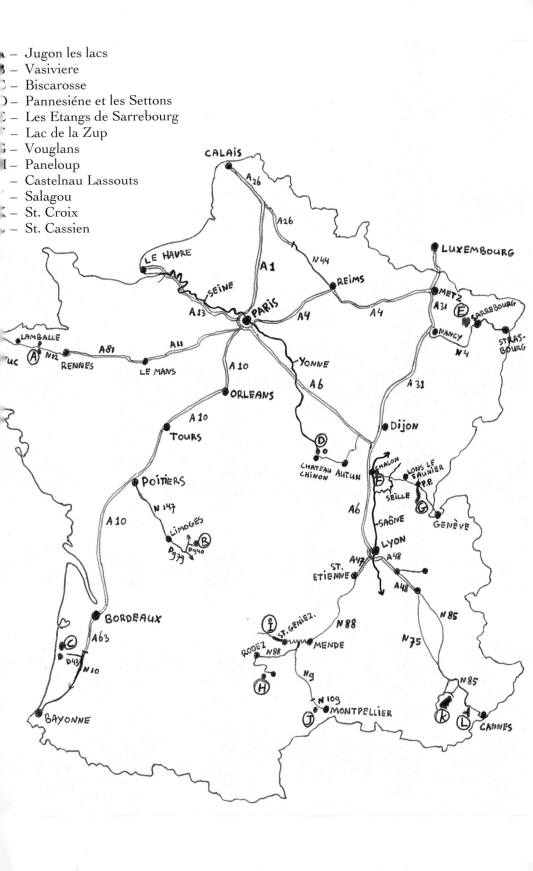

A – Jugon les lacs
B – Vasiviere
C – Biscarosse
D – Pannesiéne et les Settons
E – Les Etangs de Sarrebourg
F – Lac de la Zup
G – Vouglans
H – Paneloup
  – Castelnau Lassouts
  – Salagou
K – St. Croix
L – St. Cassien

*The Upper River Doubs.*

# Tour de France

Leon has already made a selection of 28 carp waters in various parts of France. Here I will attempt to pinpoint waters for the all-round angler, concentrating mainly on the more popular species.

Before I begin, I will list weights of some large specimens landed in France: Carp - 81½lb; Barbel - 15½lb; Bream - 10½lb; Pike - 45lb+; Catfish - 200lb; Blackbass - 6lb+; Perch - 5½lb; Zander - 30lb+; Salmon - 36lb+; Tench - 8lb+; Trout - river 22½lb, lake 31lb+; Sea trout - 17lb+; Rudd - 3lb+; Roach - 5¼lb.

As you can see, there are quite good specimens to be had, so let's cross that strip of ship-infested salt water and plant our feet on French soil, at Calais.

There are a number of canals in this area offering good mixed fishing. One of the best is the Colme canal, 9km south of Dunkerque, with carp to 24lb+. Good zander to 26lb+ (!) have been caught where the Colme canal joins the river Aa, at Watten.

Driving south west on the A26 motorway, we come to St. Quentin. Here lies the St. Quentin canal which connects to the Sambre and Oise canals and the Oise river. It contains many 20lb+ carp up to 35lb+. Pike have been landed to over 30lb in the canal further north at Cambrai.

Just 25km west of St. Quentin lies the Somme canal at Peronne. The best places to fish are at Frise and the back-arm lake at Cléry.

The river Moselle, just south of Metz is a good carp river, producing specimens to 39lb+; the best area lies between Corny and Pagny. The Rhine backwaters around Strasburg hold large catfish, carp and pike.

By taking the B300 north of Strasburg, we come to the Staelly reservoir at Soufflenheim with good pike, and carp to 40lb.

The wonderful river Doubs begins its journey along the Swiss border before bending back on itself and tumbling through beautiful countryside until it joins the river Saone at Verdun. This is one of my favourite French barbel rivers and it holds a host of other species. The upper reaches around Morteau offer mainly good chub and trout fishing.

At Malbuisson, south of Pontarlier, lies the St. Point lake and is one of France's better pike waters, with some very large specimens present amongst many other species.

*Long lean wildie-like commons inhabit the French rivers.*
*The River Ain above Vouglans Lake.*

Just east of Morteau at the base of Mt. Chatelard, the river Doubs has been dammed to form the Brenet/Chaillexon lake which stretches for 7km and holds good carp, tench, pike, bream, perch and chub. The river rushes out of the Chatalo dam and cuts its way through a long gorge, brushing the Swiss border, and this is a great place for big trout and grayling.

Another dam at Vaufrey (just above St. Hippolyte) holds up the river once again and here good carp, bream and zander can be had.

The Rhine/Rhône canal runs alongside the Doubs below Montbeliard until they both join at l'Isle. This is a great place to base yourself; I will never forget the first time I visited this area and drove my 850cc motor bike along the N83 road under a blazing sun, with the Doubs sparkling its way down the valley towards Clerval and Baume. The good thing about this area is that you can choose to fish the slow moving stretches for carp to 30lb+ and pike over 20lb, or the fast stretches for barbel into double figures and chub up to 6lb.

10km south of Verdon (west of Metz) on the D34 road, lie three medium sized rectangular shaped lakes next to the river Meuse, all holding 20lb+ carp.

If we carry on down the D34 to St. Mihiel, then take the small D119 road through Woinville, we come to the huge Madine lake. This is a good pike fishery, with many fish over 30lb.

The 901/35 roads south west of Madine take us to St. Dizier. South of St. Dizier, at Eclaron, is the massive Der-Chantecog lake. This water holds very big pike, carp and zander. The area directly south of the lake is drained by a number of good chub and trout streams which all flow into the Voire river. The Voire has produced a number of double figure barbel. The best area is between Rosnay (on the D396) and Chalette (D35), just before it joins the Aube river.

The river Aine begins its journey not far from the source of the Doubs and winds its way through lovely countryside until it reaches the Rhone river at Anthon. At Chambly village the river runs through two lakes, both holding good trout, carp, tench and pike.

Further downstream, just north of Doucier, lies the big Chalain lake. It holds pike up to 35lb and carp over 30lb, with some over 40lb, and large zander and bream.

Downstream of Doucier, the river runs into Blye reservoir. This is a beautiful water, with cliffs along one edge and meadows and woods on the other. With reeds and arrowhead lilies in the margins, it sets a lovely atmosphere to get away from it all and float fish for the big tench and carp that bubble along the margins in the early mornings. The head of fish is not large for the acreage, but the size of some of the tench makes it well worth while. Remember, no fishing is allowed inside the wildlife reserve markers at the southern end.

Between Blye and Pont-de-Poitte, the river runs into Vouglans lake. Apart from the very good carp fishing already mentioned by Leon, this large water also holds pike to over 35lb, trout to over 20lb, perch to 5lb and zander to over 20lb.

5km further downstream the river flows into another lake at Chancia. This is a lovely looking water with good pike and carp over 30lb.

Catfish have colonised a number of the river Saône's tributaries, especially around the small village of Ratenelle on the river Seille. A good area for cats on the Saône is between Mácon and Villefranche. A 78$\frac{1}{2}$lb catfish was landed in the summer of 1989 at St. Georges de Reneins, 10km north of Villefranche.

Further downstream at St. Germain au mt. d'Or, a 55 pounder was landed. (See 'Catfish Paradise' for further information on big cats).

The river Allier is another good river with specimens of many species. Carp to over 30lb have turned up at Issoir.

Another good area is at St. Germain des-Fosses, north of Vichy.

The river Lot holds good barbel (a few over 10lb), chub and trout, between Espalion and Entraygues, and above St. Geniez d'Olt. The lake below St. Geniez is known for its good carp fishing, but it also holds pike to 30lb+ and zander over 20lb. Large zander to 25lb have also been caught at St. Livrade, just 9km downstream of Villeneuve.

By taking the D920 road north from Espalion, we come to Aurillac. 10km west of Aurillac, the Cére river has been dammed to form the St. Etienn-Cantales reservoir. This lovely stretch of water with four main arms, contains perch over $3\frac{1}{2}$lb, 20lb+ zander, pike to 35lb+ and numerous 20lb+ carp with a few over 40lb.

*Jean Pierre Poulalier with a 63lb catfish from Seille.*

*Famous French carp angler Didier Cottin with a lovely $30^{1/}{}_2$lb common from Aveyron.*

If we take the N120 from Aurillac to Tulle and then the D978 through Clergoux, we come to the Valette reservoir at Marcillac. This large water holds many pike over 20lb, with some over 30lb, and good zander and carp.

The Garonne river holds numerous species. Large pike and zander over 20lb have been caught at Grenade, 25km north of Toulouse.

The Biscarrose and Etang de Parentis lakes mentioned in the carp chapter, also hold very big bream, and zander to 28lb!

We now move over to the south eastern area of France.

The Rhone holds good cats and carp along its length. The Ardéche tributary holds large barbel and chub along the 40km long gorge below Vallon-Pont-d'Arc. The river Aigues above Orange is a nice river to fish for barbel (to 7lb+) and chub, but make sure you don't fish during holidays, as the place will be swarming with picnickers and bathers! (Be warned - this can happen at many places during the French summer holidays).

Lake Cassien (west of Cannes), is noted for its huge carp, but many people don't realise that the water also holds 20lb+ zander, large blackbass, big eels and, of course, that fantastic 200lb catfish (how many more like that swim around, I wonder?).

If we travel west from Cassien on the N7 road and turn off at Flassons, then drive north along the D13 (with the lovely Issole river escorting us all the way),

*Lake Vouglans has turned up some very impessive big perch, like this lovely fish.*

we come to the Carces lake, just 5km after Cabasse. Both the Carami and Issole rivers run into this lovely 4.2km long, 244 acre water with maximum depths of 16 metres, although average depths are around 18-20 feet. This lake holds zander to 28lb+, good blackbass, perch to 4lb+ and pike over 20lb. It is also a decent carp water, with at least ten fish landed over 30lb and some to over 45lb.

We now travel back up north to Tours on the rivers Loire and Cher. The Cher holds barbel into double figures (average 3-6lb), big chub, and zander to over 15lb. The best area is just downstream of Thesée (8km east of Montrichard), where the river splits into two.

Further upstream, at St. Aignan, the river flow is much slower and is a good place for carp, roach and pike.

South west of Tours and 21km south of Thouars on the D938 road, lies the 418 acre, 4km long, Cebron reservoir. The lake averages about 20 feet in depth, with 60ft at the dam wall. It holds many carp over 20lb, double figure zander (but many small ones also), perch to 3lb+ and many pike, with some reaching 30lb.

The town of Angers is a good place to base yourself for a family holiday. Here the rivers Sarthe, Loir, Authinon and Mayenne all join the grand river Loire to produce a fantastic complex of streams and backwaters in a very small area. Large carp, bream, zander, roach, chub, barbel and eels can be caught here. Large chub and barbel are best sought out on the Meyenne river around Le Lion.

South of Paris, along the N91 between Mennecy and la Ferté-Alais, lie a number of small lakes along the river Essone, all holding large carp and pike. The river Essone itself is a very good barbel river, including the Juine tributary. Near the town of Etampes a $13\frac{1}{2}$lb barbel was caught in 1989.

A good place on the Seine is the lake at Laacourt (take the D147 north of Mantes on the western side of Paris), with big pike, carp, tench and chub.

Vernon, 20km downstream, is also a good area for carp, including the backwaters at Muids and Poses (downstream of les Andelys), with many 'bags' of 20lb+ carp landed.

# Monster Carp

The reason France has become the most popular country for holiday carp anglers is, of course, because of the many reports of enormous carp which have been caught over the last ten years or so. Most of you who come to France are dreaming of hooking (and landing of course!) a true monster, a fish in the 50-70lb region, while some of you are even searching for a, as yet undiscovered, paradise containing record size carp (70-100lb).

But let's face reality; by now thousands of European carp anglers have been pioneering in hundreds of French waters and, as far as I know, St. Cassien is still the only French lake which has produced numbers of true monster carp. On the other hand, perhaps only a quarter of all French waters are seriously fished for big carp, and none of them are receiving angling pressure comparable to Cassien.

Perhaps some have already discovered a super 'lac' but are keeping quiet about it. I know people who are fishing in France regularly but refuse to tell anything about their experiences. This I can understand; they've gone to a lot of trouble to find a special water and I would react in the same way if I knew such a water. In fact, I could list quite a lot of waters here which, in theory, could produce really huge carp, but I won't, because this would spoil everything. After all, the satisfaction of pioneering is in discovering it all on your own, or with some friends. Naming any water would, in no time, result in the water being hammered and this I want to avoid at any price!

However, the fact is that perhaps 90% of those fishing French waters are struggling, and half of them are even struggling to catch a nice fish! Often they are fishing a water of which they have heard rumours of big fish (I myself have made the same mistake in the past), others are fishing waters which are reputed to be so-called carp waters.

The Castalnau lake at St. Geniez d'Olt is a good example of this. Although the lake produces a few carp to 40lb, it's heavily overstocked with small carp (mainly commons, with a few mirrors, between 5 and 15lb). The few bigger fish in this water are those left of an older population which lived there before the (too) heavy stockings took place in the eighties. The lake is certainly on its 'retour' now. I visited this lake in May 1989 to inspect the situation, but was unimpressed by what I saw. In a small area of the lake I saw up to 500 small carp jumping every evening! To catch a bigger fish you'll have to fish through dozens, perhaps hundreds of small carp, so the really big one will be a lucky goal.

Half the surrounding woods at this lake are dead, because of pollution and the water level is changing all the time. When the water level is rising, some parts of the lake become unfishable because of dead trees floating in the water! In spite of this, in summer the place becomes pretty crowded with Dutch and English anglers (sometimes fighting for a swim I've heard!). However, I would like to recommend this lake to people who like to have loads of runs, but certainly not to the real pioneering specimen hunter.

Now, where was I? Oh yeah, monster carp...

Waters like the Castalnau lake are not likely to produce real monster carp - there are simply too many carp in these waters and the top weight of some carp in these waters is about 40lb (old carp which lived there before the lake's population exploded!).

What you should look for are lakes which are rich in natural food and hold a small population of carp. Food is not the only important factor in producing monster carp; another factor is the age of the lake and the time the first stocking took place, and with this we come to what could be the main problem of the situation in France.

The lakes which are most likely to produce really huge carp are the so called 'lacs de barrages' which are formed by damming a river. Many of these lakes are only about 20 years old (1968-1972), and are extremely rich in natural food. Some of these E.D.F. lakes I **know** were only stocked with carp about 17-18 years ago, and are already producing fish in excess of 50lb! If we look back at the situation on lake Cassien ten years ago, the biggest carp caught were in the 50lb region! Within five years or so, I can see a number of lakes producing carp of the Cassien-stamp (or bigger!).

Now, knowing these facts, you'll realise that instead of fishing everywhere (and catching nowhere), it's far better to select one or two of these rich E.D.F. lakes and concentrate on these waters in the years to come, to learn how to fish the water. This is what I'm doing now and I'm sure to be rewarded with some exceptional fish in the near future. Perhaps I'm very optimistic, but only time will tell.

The climate is, of course, another important factor. In a warmer climate the fish will feed for twelve months of the year, and lakes in warmer climates are generally richer in natural food. This combination results in fish growing faster. On the other hand, if the climate is too hot the carp will do too well and there will be an explosion in propagation which, in turn, means that the water becomes overstocked with small carp as we can see in many waters in Spain, Africa, U.S.A. etc., etc. Given the right climatic conditions carp will grow faster and become bigger and it seems that France has about the ideal climate.

In this chapter I've given you my own (optimistic) opinion about monster carp in France, but some people do not share the same opinion. I discussed the matter with Didier Cottin and his opinion was that even when all the important factors are in line, this still doesn't guarantee monster carp and that the situation at Cassien still remains a mystery. He's been fishing older waters in the south of France, which are equally rich in natural food as Cassien (crayfish), but they don't produce the numbers of monster carp that Cassien does. This means that the enormous crayfish population in Cassien isn't the main factor in producing the monster carp.

*Above: Didier Cottin with a superb French brace of a 43$\frac{1}{2}$lb mirror and a 32$\frac{1}{2}$lb common.*
*Below: Lake St. Cassien – the area known as the spawning bay*

In the region of Chalon, I know some smaller, understocked lakes which contain enormous crayfish populations but the carp in these waters are not showing exceptional growth rates compared to other lakes. It seems that the key factor in producing monster carp is still unknown. Could it be that even when a lake is rich in natural food the carp sometimes don't profit from this potential?

I first started thinking about this theory after I was confronted with some inexplicable differences in behaviour of carp living in comparable environments. I'm talking about three local lakes that I fished with some friends in the summer of '88. The lakes have all the same age, form, dimension, depth, bottom, density of carp, natural food sources etc., etc., and were stocked in the same years with carp of the same size ($^3/_4$lb) from the same fish farm (propagation never took place!) Even the chemical composition of these waters has to be the same as they are all flooded occasionally by the same river! Now, here comes the mystery: lake A only produced carp in the margins during the evening and night; lake B produced carp at distance during the day and in the margins at night, while lake C only produced at distance during both day and night. We fished the waters with the same baits and methods and these lakes have never received angling pressure before, so the carp were behaving in a natural way. The only reason that I can think of to explain this different behaviour is that the carp in these lakes are not feeding on the same natural food sources (if we accept that we caught the carp from their natural feeding areas). This could explain why the carp didn't show the same average top weight in each lake. Lake A holds carp up to about 15lb, in lake B a number are over 30lb, while in lake C the mid-twenty region is the limit!

To put it simply, let's say that the lakes are containing two main food sources on which the carp can live. A good source - X, which is good food, and a better food - Y (more nutritious). Both food sources taste good to the carp but by coincidence, the carp, after being stocked, only learned to feed on food X. Food X is good food and the carp are feeling well by eating this so have no reason to change their behaviour. In this case the carp will show normal growth rates - lake A, but imagine that by coincidence, the carp learn to feed on food Y. This would result in better growth rates - lake C; but what if a combination of food X and Y meant an even more nutritional (balanced) diet, and the carp fed on both of these food sources? This would surely result in the carp showing exceptional growth rates - lake B.

If my theory is correct, and I can't see why it isn't, we can conclude that if all the important factors are in line, only coincidence will decide whether the situation will result in monster carp or not. The situation at Cassien could, for a part, be coincidence (as Didier believes too) but it isn't. In fact, it's **me** who caught all those whackers about ten year ago and put them in Cassien!!

Now, seriously, it becomes complicated and frustrating to find and select 'monster carp waters', and surely the main factor in finding such a water is simply **luck**, (bad luck being the big risk of pioneering).

With this we come to the end of this chapter. I only wish you courage; be confident - after all, the only sure way to unmask the secrets of a big lake is by putting enough time in on it!

Good luck!

# Dream
# Season – 1989

I'm one of those carp anglers who likes to fish new waters, and although I prefer big waters, both rivers and lakes, I also like to fish one smaller water on a regular basis. Fishing new, and often virgin waters, I can never set myself targets because I never know what can be expected; I just try to get the best results in a given situation and hope to catch some big ones. Sometimes I do, but often I struggle.

The first few months of 1989 were no exception, and by the end of April I had only managed some small carp from a lake in the south of France. The waters in my region (Saône et Loire) were still not producing carp although we had hot weather in March and the water temperatures were good.

I had been fishing a beautiful 80 acre lake with my friend Huib Rentzing and his wife Marianne, who came all the way from Holland to fish here for a week. Just after arriving on the lake it started to rain and two days later we had to leave, without a fish, because of the rising water level. When we came back the next day the rain had stopped but the water level had risen 5 feet! The surrounding woods were under water and I actually saw a carp jumping between the trees! Knowing that we had to wait for one or two weeks before we could fish the lake again, Huib and his wife returned home to Holland. By now, I had become desperate - I just wanted to catch a nice fish, even a good double would do - I had to change my plans.

The year before, I had been fishing in the first lake of a three lake complex situated in a valley not far from my home; I had many twenties up to 28lb 10oz from this lake. I had also fished the second lake a couple of times, using maize, and caught some low doubles. This second lake, a 30 acre gravel pit, is known for its small carp and locals are fishing for them with very basic methods at close range. They don't catch a lot, but if they do, they kill the fish - which is still very common in my region.

On one of my trips there, I lost a big carp, which took about 40 yards of my 15lb line from the reel before the hook pulled out, so I knew that there were some large carp in the lake, probably the same size as in the first lake, as both lakes were the same age (approximately 20 years).

In early May, I decided to do a few sessions on this second lake, hoping to catch one or two nice fish. I baited up a swim twice, with medium sized Scopex boilies at 70 yards out, where I had found a depth of only 3 feet. I was expecting carp on this plateau because they would soon be spawning.

The first session was on May 8th. I fished the whole day in nice weather but had no 'bleeps' and saw no sign of carp. I baited up the swim a few times and was back early on the morning of May 14th. My wife came with me this time. It was again nice weather and during the morning I had no action at all, so I told my wife that this was going to be my worst season ever! Then, just before noon, I had a slow take and I struck into a very powerful fish which took over 100 yards of my 10lb line from the spool before it stopped for the first time. In fact, it stopped because it was at the other end of the lake! During the rest of the fight, I was very nervous and afraid of losing the fish; I had never before experienced such a powerful fight and many times the fish took 40 or 50 yards of line from the reel while I was unable to stop it. Anyway, I didn't lose the fish and about 20 minutes later a huge carp slipped into the net and when I placed her on the bank I couldn't believe my eyes - an enormous leather carp - I had never seen such a big fish in all my life!

With my scales that go up to 44lb, we were unable to weigh her, so we sacked the fish and I sent my wife to get bigger scales, a second camera and some of my friends. While she was away, I had another run and landed a 21 pounder, after a short fight. This fish looked like a bream compared to the big one. I decided to sack this fish too, and then waited for my wife to return. She came back about one hour later with some friends of mine, to witness the fish.

We first took a photo of the 'small one' and she was quickly returned to the lake; then we measured and weighed the big one. It was 39 inches long and 52lb exactly on the scales; I had pulverised my ancient personal best by some 17lb! We took many photographs and afterwards the carp was safely returned to her home.

The next few days I was, of course, fishing the same swim again, but I was catching only mid-doubles on the medium sized boilies. In the meantime, I observed signs of big fish in the centre of the lake and discovered that this was the holding area of the big ones during daylight hours. I decided to fish in the centre of the lake with big, $1\frac{1}{2}$ inch diameter boilies as single hookbaits, because the big fish were not very active and I didn't want to attract small carp. What a success it proved to be; in just a few short sessions I had 9 twenties (most of them 'uppers') and a thirty!

On May 31st, I was back at the lake with my wife again and I had another thirty. I remember saying to her, "I think this is going to be my best season ever!"

In early June, the carp were spawning and lost interest in my baits. After this 'love spell', I started catching carp again a few days later, this time on smaller $\frac{3}{4}$ inch boilies, in a heavily baited swim. This was a less selective method, but great fun because I was catching a lot of hard fighting carp between 15 and 20lb. By the end of June I had caught almost the whole population (with this I mean all the carp over 15lb; I didn't catch the smaller ones on boilies), so it was time to relax a bit, and to look for other waters.

In July, I planned some holiday trips to lake Vouglans in the 'Jura' (4,000 acres!), which is one of the most beautiful and peaceful lakes you can imagine.

I had heard rumours about very big carp from this lake, but these rumours proved to be inaccurate. I fished a swim in the northern part of the lake with maize and boilies and had loads of carp between 10 and 20lb, with the occasional 20lb+ fish.

In the same period, some friends of mine were fishing other parts of the lake and had about the same results. None of us ever saw signs of really big carp and my opinion now is that the lake is too cold, overstocked and poor in natural food. All the carp caught there, both commons and mirrors, were long, lean shaped, and certainly not of a breed capable of producing huge and heavy carp of the Cassien stamp. However, I enjoyed the fishing there, but will not return to the place in the future.

(**NB**. *Leon actually visited Vouglans for a last 'crack' at the big fish in May, 1990, but landed only lean looking fish again, to upper twenties. S. H. from France, who has fished Vouglans for the last 7 years, wrote me a letter giving details of commons he had caught over 45lb and also witnessed the capture and took photographs of the so-called 96 pounder - a fish that was, apparently, 88lb in July, 1989, 90lb in September, 93lb in December, and 96lb in 1990! After writing back to S. H. and after Leon had spoken to S. H. in May, 1990, I am now of the same opinion as Leon.* **Tony**).

Although at the end of 1989 I never thought to go back to the lake, I changed my mind in 1990. Why? Because I had loved the fishing over there. The place was peaceful and the fishing was simple, pure. I didn't go back to catch a biggie but just to have a bend in the rod. Yes, size is relative at times, even for me!

Anyway, I went back there three times in 1990. I had one very successful session (low water level) and two blanks (high level and dropping level!). I met quite a lot of carp anglers over there that year and saw many, many carp on the bank plus a large number of pictures of carp from the lake were shown to me (the total number of carp I'm talking about is far over one thousand!) and I can now make the following conclusions:

About 15% of all these fish were between 5 and 10lb.

75-80% were between 10 and 20lb.

5-10% were over 20lb.

2-3% were over 25lb.

1% were over 30lb (up to 37lb).

The lake also produced one **exceptional** carp of 55lb, caught at long distance in over 60 feet of water (near Largillay). Fish of 46 and 49.5lb are claimed to have been caught in the same area but I still haven't seen a picture of these fish.

In 1990 the lake produced a lot more big carp than in preceding years and boilies are working better and better. Fishing seems to be a lot better with low water levels, which is logical as both the lake's natural food stock and the total surface of the lake are considerably reduced. Best months for big fish (25lb+) were May and June. However, fish of over 35lb, although existing, are still very rare.

The final conclusion would be that Vouglans, although being an exceptional lake on its own can, in no way, be compared with lakes such as St. Cassien or Les Etangs de Sarrebourg, which are all reputed to hold large numbers of big carp.

Next year I'll go back and hope for a thirty!

More about Vouglans in the next edition.

August arrived and I did some fun fishing in the Saône and a local lake, catching carp up to about 20lb. By the end of the month I was fed up with catching doubles and returned to the 'valley' for some big carp. I wanted to catch a big mirror of about 40lb that I had seen on two occasions, but had not yet caught. I also hoped to catch the big leather again because the photographs I had of it were of poor quality. In a few short sessions I caught some known twenties on peanut ethyl alcohol flavoured 1 inch boilies.

On September 14th, I caught the big leather which, without spawn but in perfect condition, weighed almost 48lb this time, so I had my photographic revenge.

A few days later I found out that the big mirror I was after had been caught and killed by a French angler; she weighed 31lb without head and intestines!! I was very sad about this and want to point out here that I'm very disappointed with the fact that the French angling press are not making enough effort to promote the 'no kill mentality' and stop showing pictures of proud anglers with big, dead fish in their magazines every month. I feel that the French angling press have a great responsibility concerning the evolution to the right side, but unfortunately they are ignoring this responsibility and continuing their stupid policies in the wrong way - very sad indeed!

But let me continue the story...

It was time to leave the valley and try other waters, in search of big carp. It was late September by now (time for the big ones), and after some visits to different lakes, I chose a 400 acre gravel pit 20 miles from my home. The lake had been stocked with carp 20 years ago, but nobody was fishing for them any more. About 50% of the lake was filled with massive weed beds, full of insect larvae and crayfish - a real paradise for greedy carp - so I expected big fish.

The swim I chose was a clear area of about 30 yards wide, between two enormous weed beds, at 100 yards+ from the bank. The depth was 7ft (the deepest part of the lake), and the bottom was hard and clean. The idea was to intercept the carp which were travelling from one weed bed to the other; I also hoped to keep the carp in the baited swim during the winter after the weed had died.

I did two short sessions with small, strawberry flavoured boilies, but was

*Dream Season! Leon with the leather on its second capture: 47lb 15oz*

*A big brace for Leon*

having a lot of problems with the small catfish, which kept attacking my baits until they finally hooked themselves. To solve this problem, I changed to rock hard 1 inch boilies, with a more neutral pH flavour. I baited up the swim a few times (200 boilies per day), and decided to do short sessions (5-8 hours) until the end of the year.

I was catching big carp right from the start; the first seven sessions produced 7 twenties and 5 thirties, which proves that it isn't always necessary to live for many days in a stinking bivvy to catch some big carp. It's just a matter of logical thinking, good planning and timing. I will describe the two most memorable sessions:

**7.10.89.**

I arrived at the lake at half past seven in the morning. The day before I had caught mirrors of 14.06 and 23.10 and a third fish had cut the line just a few seconds after striking. It had been raining all day and night but today the rain had stopped, although it was still very cloudy. I catapulted about 100 baits into the swim at 100 yards+, which wasn't too difficult, with a strong wind blowing on my back. At 8 o' clock the three rods were in position, so I put the kettle on and sat back in my car which was parked just a few yards from my rods. I had a cuppa, smoked a cigarette and turned on the radio to listen to the weather forecast at 9 o' clock.

Just before nine, one of the rods was away and a few seconds later I was hanging on to the rod. A powerful carp took about 20 yards of line from the spool before it buried itself into a massive weed bed about 120 yards out. All went solid. I tried all the tricks, but the fish didn't move an inch so I placed the rod back on its rests with the baitrunner on, and observed the spot where the carp was snagged, with my binoculars.

After ten minutes or so, the whole weed bed started to move; the baitrunner was clicking - first slowly, then faster and faster. I took the rod and pulled as hard as I dare, then I saw the end of the line moving to the left. The carp was free and in open water now. Fifteen minutes later, a big leather slipped into the net. After closer inspection on the bank, I saw that it had a second hook, with a short hooklink in its mouth, so it must have been the same fish that I had lost the day before. She went 33lb exactly. I sacked her to show her to my friends who had promised to visit me in the early afternoon.

I cast the rod back into position and one hour later I caught a smaller fish after a one minute battle - a mirror of 17.10, which I put back immediately. At noon, I had a lovely 19lb mirror, which I also sacked, then the swim went dead.

Until 3 o'clock, I saw no signs of carp, then my friend came and I told him what had happened in the morning. We took some photographs of the two carp and put them back in the lake. After a cup of coffee we were surprised by another screaming run and after a powerful fight my friend landed a big mirror for me, which we both thought to be heavier than the leather, but we were wrong, she went 31.15. This was the last fish of the day and at 5 o'clock I packed up and returned home with a smile on my face.

## 24.10.89.

Although it was now late October, the weather was still very nice, with temperatures in the seventies. I had been fishing a lot and my wife was complaining that I didn't spend enough time with her. I explained to her that she was lucky to be married to a carp angler, instead of a man who spends the whole day long hanging around bars and drinking 'pastis'. I told her that the month of October was the period for the big ones and that I simply must go fishing, it was a force stronger than me. The expression on her face told me that it didn't work! "Listen darling, it will soon be winter and too cold to go fishing, so let me go again a few times; I'll be back at 5 o'clock and we'll have a romantic evening together."

"Mmmmm...", she said. I kissed her and was away.

I was at the lake at seven o'clock in the morning and again, there were no anglers. It was going to be a nice sunny day without wind, so I put my bedchair behind the rods. At half past seven my rods were out. I had put approximately 100 baits into the swim and I knew that I was going to catch some carp. The last six sessions had all produced twenties and/or thirties. I had so much confidence that I had already lined out a sack and taken my scales and weigh sling out of the car!

I laid back on my bedchair and was looking at the rod tips. Between 7.30 and 8 o'clock, some big fish rolled over the baits. Just after 8.00 one of the rod tips was making silly movements, but no line was taken from the spool, and the Optonic gave just one bleep. Ten seconds later, the same thing happened again. I struck immediately and made contact with a fish that swam very fast towards me. I wound in as quickly as possible, but the fish managed to reach a massive weedbed 30 yards from the bank and about 50 yards out; then all went solid. I could see the fish on the surface and it looked very big. I tried the same method as described before - rod on the rests and baitrunner on. About ten minutes later the fish moved and took some line, so I picked up the rod and pulled very hard. Suddenly, 'ping' - a line cut and a big bow-wave. "Bad luck", I thought, and wound in the rod, put on another rig and bait, then cast back into position.

At ten o' clock, I had a run and caught 'Le Goulue', a well known 19 pounder (mirror), which I had already caught four times on previous trips, and even my wife had caught it once. "Hard luck", I thought, and recast all three rods and rebaited with about 50 boilies.

After this I saw no more activity, but at half past two I again had a run which produced a lovely mirror of 24.12. I sacked this fish and again recast the rods and rebaited with 50 boilies.

At four o' clock, some pike anglers showed up at the lake and fished a swim about 100 yards to the right of me. I went to see one of them and asked him if you could take some photographs of me and the fish. He came with me, took some pictures, and was very surprised when he saw me putting the fish back into the lake.

It was quarter to five by now and I had to pack up, for I had promised my wife that I would be back by 5 o' clock.

As I went to pick up the first rod, I was surprised by a very fast run and after a hectic battle I landed a big leather of 37lb 8oz. The pike angler, who was still with me, again took some photos and when I put the fish back into the water, the second rod was away and produced a powerful 21 pounder (mirror). Again, some photos were taken and believe it or not, after returning this fish, the third rod was away and produced the smallest carp of the day - a 17lb mirror.

I came back home at seven o' clock in the evening and my wife was waiting for me with a cold dinner. She looked into my eyes and waited for an explanation. I was smiling.

"How many, one or two?" she asked.

"Five!" I said. "Up to seventeen kilos."

Suddenly, a big smile appeared on her face; she was happy for me.

"Can you warm up my dinner for me?" I asked.

"Of course, my love," she said.

She's really fantastic. By the way, we had a very romantic evening...

Early November, the summer was over now. After a few days with heavy rainfall, the temperatures dropped drastically. In the next four sessions the action slowed down. I had only five carp, including 'Le Goulue' again, and two unknown mid-twenties.

On November 11th, the water temperature was only 39°F., whilst the week before it was still 54°F., so I decided to wait until the night frosts had stopped before giving it a try again.

For the rest of November we had extremely cold weather, which is exceptional for my region, and by the end of the month the lakes were frozen over. It was mid-December when the temperatures climbed up to the low fifties and as soon as the ice was gone, I did a last session but blanked in an awful hurricane.

**Conclusions.**

I ended the year with the following results. Over one hundred and forty carp, including forty twenties, seven thirties, an upper forty and a low fifty! All my 20lb+ carp, but one, were caught during daylight hours! I spent about 900 hours fishing, half of which were especially for the big ones. That might seem a lot, compared to the results, but I spend more time in the preparation - about 1,000 hours preparing baits and travelling to new waters in search of big carp.

I rolled over 25,000 big boilies with my hands! I've found this to be the only method to make perfect round baits, which are essential to prebait a swim accurately at 120 yards with a catapult. I didn't fish with boilies over particles, which seems to be the most popular method these days. Having fished with this method for a couple of years, I'm now sure that this is certainly not the best method of selecting big carp, and I had far better results fishing with boilies over boilies, or as single hookbaits. To explain why this is, I will describe the good and bad points of each method.

**Boilies over a large bed of particles:**
*Good Points:*
It's not an expensive method and the preparation is easy. In large waters (barrages, rivers) with nomadic carp, it's often the only method to hold the carp in a swim for some hours.
*Bad Points:*
The particles will attract many small carp and other species. Catching a small carp will disturb the swim and reduce the chances of catching a big fella. If the water doesn't hold many small carp and some big ones are feeding in the swim, they will often become preoccupied on the particles and ignore the boilies, even a pop up!

Under such circumstances it's better to fish with particles as hookbait.

*Leon with the big leather of 52lb*

149

## Boilies over boilies:

*Good Points:*

Doesn't attract small carp (I'm only talking about hard boilies of at least 18mm diameter). The feeding carp in the swim will only search for boilies, which is also the hookbait. This will result in more, and confident, runs. Prebaiting at long distance is possible without the use of a boat.

*Bad Points:*

It's a more expensive method (depending on the mix you use) and needs a lot of preparation.

## Boilies as single hookbaits:

*Good Points:*

A cheap method with the minimum of preparation. If a big bait is used (1½ inch), only big carp will be able to take it (very selective!). This method worked for me when the carp were absolutely passive and no other anglers had any action, yet my single hookbait, fished in a known holding area, produced carp, although I doubt if the carp had any intention of eating my bait; perhaps they were just playing with that big, strange, yellow, nice smelling ball!

*Bad Points:*

Can only be used under circumstances where the big fish can be localised exactly (you can't attract them with only one bait).

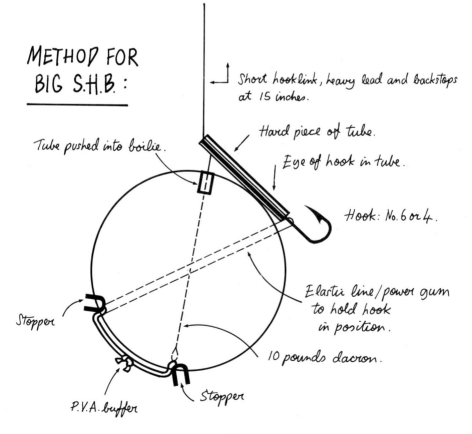

METHOD FOR BIG S.H.B. :

Short hooklink, heavy lead and backstops at 15 inches.

Hard piece of tube.

Tube pushed into boilie.

Eye of hook in tube.

Hook: No. 6 or 4.

Elastic line/power gum to hold hook in position.

10 pounds dacron.

Stopper

P.V.A. buffer

Stopper

150

I'm still at the experimental stage of fishing with very big boilies, but I could imagine that a baiting campaign with really big boilies, in a known feeding and/or holding area, is the best method of selecting very big carp. (**N.B.** I agree with Leon 100% on this point and know that Jens Bursell and others (such as Robin Monday) are of the same opinion. Tony)

I fished my big, single hookbaits in combination with tight lines to avoid twitches and didn't always have full-blooded runs, but striking on a shaking rod top also proved to be a successful method.

Drennan Super Specialist hooks, No. 6 worked well for me. I use this hook also for other methods and it never lets me down; it's very strong and sharp and when first testing this hook, only 2 carp came off out of over 70 hooked and landed.

I make my big single hook baits hard enough to resist casting but soft enough to come off during the fight. A piece of P.V.A. string fixed between the elastic and Dacron hair will work as a buffer when powerful casting is necessary (see drawing). Flavours and/or attractors should be at much lower levels than those used in 'normal' sized boilies, because a 'big' boilie will release more, due to its larger surface area and therefore a 'normal' level may be too strong to be acceptable to the fish.

This year I was surprised by the potential of some smaller waters (gravel pits) in my region, and reading the French angling press I came across many reports of very big carp (50lb+) from small waters. This is not strange if you know that these smaller and often shallow waters contain many weedbeds and big populations of crayfish. The carp in these waters are living in real havens of carp food and can grow unrestrained, without stress because nobody is fishing for them.


**The Future.**

How far can you go in setting yourself targets when living in France? I really don't know yet. However, as I explained before, I don't set myself targets, although I have some future ambitions. I will continue searching for a water that contains some carp of the Cassien stamp.

My dream is to catch a 60lb+ carp and a 40lb common. I would also like to catch one of those monster catfish (up to 200lb) that live in the river Saône, but that's another story.

# Future Catfish Paradise in France

*Mr Bert holds his 101$^{1}/_{2}$lb catfish from the River Seille.*

It all started in June 1977, when Mr. Bessard caught, by chance, a 25kg catfish in his square net. The fish came from a small river which is connected to the river Seille.

Two years later, Jean-Pierre Poulalier caught two smaller specimens (9 and 11kg) whilst fishing for 'poisson chat' in the Seille, which led him to believe that there had to be more, and bigger, cats in this river - so he took the decision to go and fish for them seriously.

Since then he has caught over 200 cats up to 42kg (92$\frac{1}{2}$lb), which makes him the most successful and experienced catfish angler in the region.

In the early 80's, others started to follow his example and the river Seille produced many catfish of all sizes up to 52kg (114$\frac{1}{2}$lb). In the mid eighties the river Saône started to produce cats as well; first by chance, to some pike and zander anglers, but soon after the catfish hunters followed and they caught many very big cats (between 88lb and 136$\frac{1}{2}$lb). Most people are now convinced that the river holds catfish to over 100 kilos (220lb+)!!

In '88 and '89, the pressure started to count on the small river Seille and fewer cats were caught, but of a better average size. However, the big river Saône is capable of supporting heavier angling pressure and at this moment the river is being fished seriously at only a few points between Lyon and Chalon, whilst it is a fact that big cats are living throughout the whole length of the river.

La Saône, a real 'virgin' catfish paradise which will surely become very popular in the near future.

Nobody knows exactly where they came from, but who cares? The fact is, they are there, just waiting to be caught. I will go for them this summer and I hope to catch my share.

In order to learn as much as possible about the Saône cats, I would like to ask people who have caught cats, or know of cats that have been caught, to write to me about their experiences. In exchange, I will write them a letter with all the detailed information that I have about the Saône catfish.

My address is: L. Hoogendijk, 2 RUE MENDES, 71100 SEVREY, FRANCE.

*Didier Cottin with four carp weighing between 24lb and 19lb.*

# Didier Cottin Interview

In October 1988, an International Carp Fishing Concourse was organised to promote modern carp fishing in France.

The concourse (48 hours non-stop fishing match) took place on the banks of Le Lac de la ZUP in Chalon sur Saône and was attended by 120 anglers from different countries. Although few carp were caught (up to 35lb!), the event turned out to be a success and quite a lot of people in my region have adopted the modern fishing style and, more importantly, the mentality, since.

It was during this concourse that I met Didier Cottin for the first time and I found that he was a very nice and intelligent chap.

Didier lives in Auribeau sur Siagne, which is near lake Cassien, and he had come to Chalon to join the concourse. We had a very interesting conversation about (of course) big carp, and after a while he showed me some photograph albums. I was deeply impressed by what I saw; this was the most incredible 'big carp photo collection' that I had ever seen in my life, with huge carp from St. Cassien and other lakes in the south. Didier is now one of the most successful big carp hunters in France. He recently finished his first book (September, 1989) and I'm sure you will hear much more of him in the near future.

While I was writing the articles about carp fishing in France, I thought an interview with Didier would certainly enhance the special about France. Didier lives about 350 miles from my home and we couldn't arrange a meeting in time, so I sent him the questions and he sent me back a letter, with the answers, a few days later. Almost the entire letter is printed below, so here is an interview with a French big carp hunter. Read on...

31st August, 1989.

Salut Leon,

Your letter has arrived on 'the planet carp' and I proffer, having a little spare time, to write you the answers, because tomorrow we're on the way to lake Salagou and afterwards we'll go to St. Croix. We will be fishing for two weeks. I have just come back from a 15 days' fishing trip to Aveyron and St. Cassien.

After Salagou I'll go to the Sapel (International exposition of fishing tackle) in Paris and after, in late September, I'll probably go fishing in St. Cassien with some friends. Indirectly, I think I've already answered one of your questions, the one concerning my fishing hours per year.

I will try to answer your questions, and hope you like the answers.

Q. *What is your age?*
A. I was born 19.9.58. in Paris, so I'll be 31 years old in September, 1989.

Q. *When did you start carp fishing and did you fish for other species?*
A. I started carp fishing in 1981, just a few times a year. Most of the time I had line cuts; in 1981 the monsters of St. Cassien fooled me time after time. In 1982 I took my revenge and, thanks to classic methods, I caught my first big carp a **54lb** and a **35½lb** followed by other carp between 10 and 30lb.

It was the beginning of a long, enduring obsession. My thoughts were often disturbed by awful nightmares in which monster carp emptied my spools, leaving me behind with frustrations. However, it was really difficult to get away from my old passion, match fishing - fishing for zander, pike, perch and trout, for which I've been fishing since the age of 5 years.

It was not until 1984, when the first English carp anglers came to Cassien, that the obsession transformed into something which was stronger than anything else, something incurable!

Q. *What do you like the most in carp fishing?*
A. What I like the most in carp fishing is carp! What a wonderful and mysterious fish; it makes you forget the long days of waiting for a run when the fish suddenly shows herself with force on the other end of the line. What is more magic than a screaming clutch and the fact that during the fight you're not sure who will win? Of course, I like the peaceful surroundings as well as the friendships I make whilst practising this hobby, but first of all, I love carp.

Q. *In my region (Chalon), most people are still fishing with classic methods and are killing their captures. How is the evolution and mentality in your region?*
A. As far as the mentality is concerned, it's difficult to compare my region with yours. Here, the English example, followed up by the local carp anglers, helped a bit in the evolution to the right side. The principal thing is that this 'snowball' meets, on its way, intelligent and reasonable people who don't kill fish unnecessarily.

Q. *How is the situation on Cassien at present and what has changed the most, compared to the last few years?*
A. As regards the present situation at St. Cassien, the fact is, there are two clans - those who are still complaining about the night fishing foreigners, and those who want to have their night fishing legalised. One thing is for sure, and that's the fact that this second group is becoming bigger and bigger. The most frustrating thing is to see the carp anglers being looked upon as law breaking vandals, while those same carp anglers put their fish back into the water in the best possible condition and those who complain are killing pike, or keeping nets full of other species in every session.

The fishing. Since 1984, the carp have become difficult to catch, only becoming active during certain periods. This is, of course, caused by the enormous fishing pressure which is unique in France. Other species are also profiting from the repeated heavy prebaiting; on some days it becomes almost impossible to fish when big bream, big tench, roach and other species, take possession of your prebaited swim.

Q. *Do you think that the biggest Cassien carp have already been caught, or are there still some even bigger, unknown monsters in the lake?*

A. Why kill the mystery of St. Cassien? I hope, of course, that there are still some record carp which will give the fight of a lifetime to some of our fishing 'brothers' in the future. However, the months of May and June are always the best periods to hope for these monsters; some of them carry up to 15lb of spawn during this period.

Q. *In your opinion, is St. Cassien unique in France?*

A. It is quite clear that in France there are many other lakes and waters which contain carp to over 50lb, but after many trials in other waters, and having had many contacts with carp anglers in other regions, one thing becomes evident - St. Cassien is **the** lake where the biggest number of monster carp are congregated, and that makes it a unique place.

Q. *How many hours do you actually fish per year?*

A. After the introduction of my letter, you'll understand that I fish a lot, especially over the last three years - over 100 days a year I think.

Q. *Can you give me the statistics about your big carp catches (in English pounds, if possible)?*

A. I skimmed through my fishing diary and will give you the thirty biggest carp that I have caught during the last three years (up to 1989), except for the two carp which I caught in 1982:

57lb, 54lb, 49lb, 44½lb, 43½lb, 42½lb, 37½lb, 37lb, 35½lb, 32lb, 31lb, 30½lb, 30½lb, 30lb, 28½lb, 27lb, 27lb, 27lb, 27lb, (the law of series!), 26½lb, 24½lb, 24½lb, 24½lb, 24lb, 23lb, 23lb, 22lb, 21½lb, and 21½lb.

*NOTE. Jealous and unsuccessful anglers might say, "I'm not impressed by all these numbers of big carp", but anglers like me, who are fishing for the big ones, are surely impressed by this! However, I'm fishing for, and writing about, 'big' carp, so no criticism please! (Leon H.)*

Q. *How do you see the future for carp fishing in France?*

A. The future for carp fishing in France? I see it in two separate parts. One part; those who think that fishing with carbon rods, Optonics and boilies will assure lot of carp; these I think will soon turn to other horizons.

The other part, those who understand that you only deserve success by gaining limitless experience; these will form the new generation of carp anglers which will, I hope, be one big family - ready to help youngsters and capable of helping to evolve things in the right direction, as you can see in some other countries.

You asked me not to be too brief in answering your questions; I hope this will do. I have to leave you now because I'm going to load my equipment in the car and I'm going to try to modify the statistics you asked for in your ninth question!

Salagou, here we come!!

Yours carperly,
Didier.

# From The Didier Cottin Scrapbook

*August 1990. Lake St. Cassien. 46lb+*

*Sylvie Cottin, 30lb. June 1990.*
*Didier in action.*

# Night Fishing in France

J. L. Bunel has recently opened a 17¼ acre lake for night fishing in France, situated approximately 120km south west of Paris and 5km from 'la Ferte Vidame' village.

The Fuysaie lake, with depths between 3-15 feet, has nice grassy banks and plenty of open swims between the trees that flank the lake.

A maximum of 14 anglers may fish at any one time and there must be at least 50 metres between each angler. Up to 4 rods may be used per angler.

It is a nice looking lake, with plenty of reeds and weed beds growing up during the summer months. There is ample parking space, an area specially provided for cooking etc., and the added luxury of toilets (a feature which is definitely needed on some hard fished English waters!).

Prices, as of July 1990, are:
24 hours - 180 Francs
48 hours - 330 Francs
72 hours - 450 Francs
extra day - 130 Francs
one week - 910 Francs

The water holds a good stock of carp between 11 pounds and 50½ pounds. These weights are correct, because Jean-Louis spoke to me on the banks of Tucholm lake in Denmark during the last Danish Carp Concourse. Jean also said that one of the best put-and-take trout fisheries in France lies only 20km away, so this area is well worth a visit while on holiday.

Reservations must be made before fishing. Contact:
J. L. Bunel,
35, bd. Arago,
75013 Paris,
Tel. 16 (1) 43 36 68 21.

A new European angling centre is opening in France on 18th May 1991, just 30km from Rennes and with good connections by ferry to St. Malo. Take the N12 auto-route out of RENNES then turn off on the N164 to St. Meen Le Grand. Take

*The sun sets over Völkermarkter Lake – Austria*

*Tony holds just one of many doubles caught in a hectic fishing spell.*

*Lake Torel nestles among beutiful scenery.*

*The beautiful Careser Lake north of Trento.*

*Many Italian lakes hold very large black bass.*
*Tony fishing a deep run on a typical mountain river.*

the O220 route through Le Losouet Sur Meu until you see signs on the right to the FISHABIL centre.

The centre complex provides hotel, restaurants, clubhouse, cinema, horse riding, animal park, tennis, etc., for the whole family and a beautiful, well stocked, 86½ acre lake lies only a few hundred metres away. This lake has been stocked with an incredible 35 tons of big fish and has been left unfished for the past 2 years. **NIGHT FISHING IS AUTHORISED.**

The fish introduced included:

| | |
|---|---|
| PIKE | up to 39½lb |
| ZANDER | up to 33lb |
| CARP | up to 57½lb |
| CATFISH | to over 280lb |

Also big tench, grass carp, black bass and even sturgeon!
(These weights were recorded in December 1990).

### Fishing licence:
Carp/catfish - 24 hours - 240 francs.
Pike/catfish - 12 hours - 800 francs. Artificial lures only.
(the reason for this quite hefty price is because of large pike being very expensive to obtain and stock in France. I have heard that it is possible to catch 20-40 pike in 12 hours here!)
Boat - 100 francs (club boat only allowed).

### Regulations:
**All** fish returned alive to water within 12 hours. Only use carp sacks. Up to 4 rods per person. Quantity of baits unlimited. Live or deadbaits prohibited. No gaffs. No fires. Green tents preferred.

In order to preserve the quality of angling, the number of anglers will be voluntarily limited. It is, therefore, recommended to make reservations.

### Contact:
Fishabil S.A. Centre, European De Peche de specimens le lac, 22230 Loscouet-sur Meu, France. Tel. Raphael Faraji on 96 25 27 66.

**Note:** When I last talked to Raphael on the phone, he said that while taking photographs for a new catalogue, he had to use seven men to hold the biggest catfish - but still had problems trying to hold it still because of its incredible strength!

*Lake Flix is one of the best catfish waters in Spain. Here a big cat gives a last powerful flick of the tail as it is drawn over the net.*

# Tour of Spain

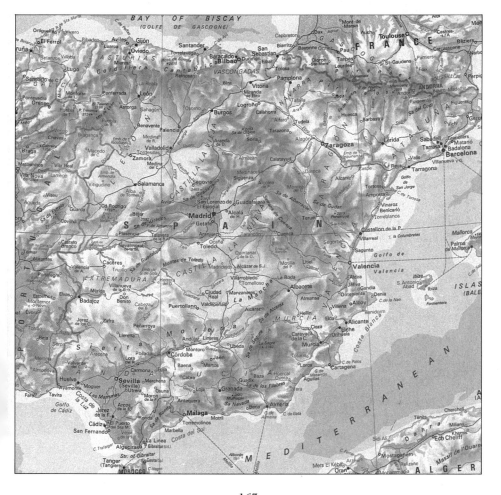

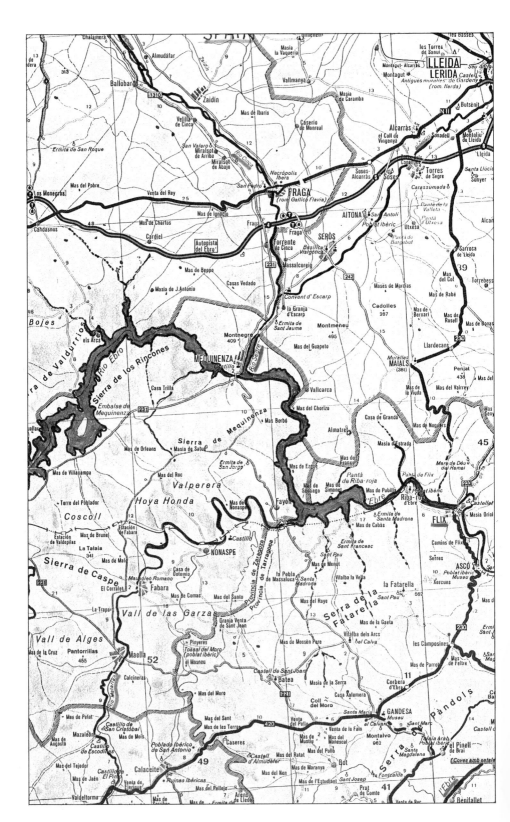

The Ebro/Ebre system:

We turn our backs on the crazy madness of Barcelona's beaches, full of pink Englishmen, and drive on the E4 motorway (or 340 road) then turn off at Amposta. Here lies the mighty Ebre delta. Between Amposta and Tortosa, in both the Ebre river and canal, big carp are caught, with some over 50lb.

The road north out of Tortosa towards Tivenys, flanks the right hand bank of the Ebre until it reaches Móra la Nova. This stretch holds large pike and chub, but is better known for its huge barbel (Barbus Capito) over 15lb, with some reaching 20lb.

Another good area for big barbel is where the Monstant river joins the Ebro just north of Móra. 20km upstream from Móra at the town of Flix, the Ebro has been dammed to form the large Flix reservoir (or Ribarroja). Fed by five rivers, this lake has grown to immense proportions and now almost joins the even larger Mequinenza reservoir upstream. Ribarroja is a wonderful carp water, containing many 10-30lb fish with some reaching 55lb. This is also a fantastic catfish water, with a good head of fish between thirty and ninety pounds, and some colossal cats over 250lb!

The Mequinenza lake is also a good water, with many species present, including large pike, trout and barbel. At the south western end of Mequinenza is the town of Caspe. The 221 road out of town crosses the Guadalope river and here is a good place for barbel.

Continuing on the 221, we cross another river, near Maella, called Materrana; here is good fishing for trout, chub and smaller barbel.

*Some Spanish waters have become so over-populated with carp due to high temperatures. On some waters you can expect catches like this one! Choose your water carefully.*

*On the other hand some waters can turn up beautiful big carp, like this superb specimen caught by Roy Stallard*

The Tajo system

Driving east on the 211 road from Alccaniz (on the river Guadalope), we turn left 5km after Molina, towards Corduente on the small mountain road. Just before Zaorejas, the road crosses at the junction of the two rivers, Tajo and Galio. Here good trout fishing is to be had with some over 5lb.

Continuing on the mountain road, we eventually meet the 320 road at Alcocer. Here lies the eastern arm of the Buendia reservoir, just part of the huge Entrepenas-Bolarque lake complex. This large lake system holds 20lb+ pike and powerful, lean wildie type carp.

We now head downstream to Toledo and enter big barbel country (Barbus Comizo). A number of rivers join the Tao in this area and all offer good fishing. The best are at the Guadarrama river junction west of town, or near the camp site at the Jaroma river junction at Aranjuez.

Heading west on the 403/E4 through Talarvera, we turn left just after Torralba on the road south to El Puente. Here the Tajo river cuts through town and is a good place to base yourself. Upstream near Aldeanueva, the river is dammed to form a long lake that stretches back to Talavera. Downstream at Peraleda, lies the Valdecanas reservoir, just one of a series of large lakes that the river flows through before entering Portugal. Upstream of El Puento and downstream near Valdelacass is a wonderful place for barbel, with some 'biggies' over 16lb landed. The Valdecanas itself holds carp, pike and chub.

*Good chub can be caught from the Guadalquivir system.*

The Guadalquivir system

The Guadalquivir drains a fantastic array of rivers and streams running off the high Sierras, before entering the great Marismas marshes south of Sevilla. The Baza, Guadalinar, Jándula and Guadelén all offer good trout fishing. The Guadalquivir offers good barbel fishing around Montoro and Andujar, with specimens to 15lb+. The stretch between Palm del Rio and Alcolea holds 20lb+ pike, carp, tench and big chub.

# Tour of Austria and Switzerland

*Spinning for pike on Afritzer Lake.*

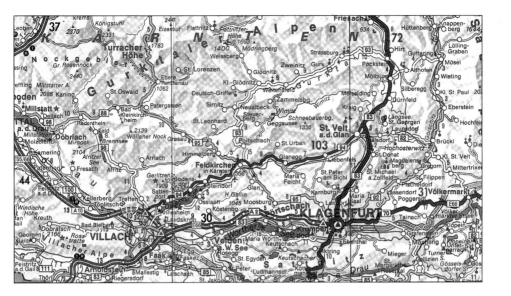

*Austria – Völkermarkter Lake, River Drau, Wörther Lake etc.*

Lands of ski lifts and St. Bernards, snow and ice, banks full of money and lakes full of fish! What, you don't believe me…? Take off those skis and drag John away from the bar and women, then follow me down the slopes into the lush, green valleys…

Vienna (Wien), that sounds romantic doesn't it? The mighty Donau cuts through its heart on its way towards the Czechoslovakian border. Route 9 flanks the river's southern bank all the way to Bratislava (Pressburg). The river Fischa breaks up into many streams after Haslach, before entering the Donau near Wildungsmauer. Here is a good place for large zander, 20lb+ pike and catfish to 35lb.

The upper reaches of the Fischa hold 'brownies' over 5lb and 'rainbows' to over 14lb. 5km downstream is a backwater or 'back arm' of the Donau where rudd to over 5½lb have been caught! It is worth mentioning at this stage the back arms of the Donau in the Vienna area; they hold 20lb+ pike, 35lb+ carp (maximum 56lb landed) and cats to over 100lb. Other good back arms are at Stopfenreuth (opposite side to Petronell) and the incredible 'octopus' system around Tulln (north west of Wien), which, besides cats and carp, produced rainbow trout to 10lb+ in 1989.

The March river follows the Austria/Czechoslovakian border before joining the Donau near Hainburg. As well as good catfish, the March holds monster asp with some reaching over 20lb!

20km south of Petronell, near Neusiedl, is the very large Neusiedler lake. On the eastern side of the lake is a nature conservancy area containing more than 70 smaller lakes. (Take the 51 road south to St. Andrä). Many of these lakes contain good pike, carp, tench and eels. One of the best is the Zick lake, with eels to 7lb+.

A number of very good tributaries of the Donau lie upstream (west) of Wien (drive along the northern bank on route 3). The Krems river, north of Krems, holds good rainbow trout and Danube salmon. The Kamp river is dammed to form the 10km long Ottenstein and the 4½km long Dobra lakes (drive north west of Krems on route 37). Both waters hold very large carp, zander, pike and good bream.

A smaller 2km long lake is formed further downstream near Idolsberg (turn north off 37 onto route 32), called Thurnberg lake, which also provides good fishing for similar species.

The river Thaya (a tributary of the Dyje/March) begins its journey just north of Offenstein lake. This river contains good trout and barbel. The best area for barbel is at Raabs, with fish up to 8lb falling for wobbled plugs!

The river Melk, south of Melk town, is another decent trout and barbel river. Good Danube salmon, grayling and trout are caught in the Enns/Steyr rivers at Steyr (south of Linz).

Just before Linz, the Traun river enters the Donau. This tributary is a good grayling river with specimens over 3lb, including chub to 5lb+, barbel and asp.

Upstream at Gmunden, the river Traun runs through the 11½km long Traun lake which holds pike over 25lb, zander, eel, tench and lake trout.

The twice as large Atter lake and adjoining Mand lake to the west of Gmunden near Seewalchen, contain similar sized species. Numerous other large lakes lie within a short radius, including Zeller, Waller, Obertstrummer, Waginger and Tachinger lakes to the west, and St. Wolfgang, Hallstätter, Altausseer and Grundl to the south, so this is obviously a good area to base yourself.

Most of these large waters hold good pike, carp, tench and catfish etc., and there are many smaller lakes to choose from, including Toplitz and Kammer lakes (east of Grund), Shwarz lake (north of Wolfgang), Abtsdorfer (south east of Oberndorf) and Heratinger lake (25km north of Oberndorfon on route 156). Many of the lakes just mentioned hold good grass carp. To give you an example, the Waller lake (near Henndorf a. Wallersee) has produced grass carp (marmor type) to 46¼lb!

A small, 12¼ acre water called Im lake on the West Germany/Austrian border, near Salzburg, holds carp over 20lb and catfish to 46lb+.

The junction of the river Mur and Pols at Lind (near Judenburg) is a fantastic area for big 'brownies' with many over 15lb and the best a fantastic 34lb+!

Further downstream at Bruck, the Murz river swells the Mur's size and here is a good area for zander (best landed in 1989 was 25lb!).

The wide and majestic Drau river holds many big fish, including Danube salmon to 80lb. Specimen Danube salmon to 44lb+ have been landed at Sachsenburg (west of Millstatter lake), and on 11th November, 1989 at 6 o' clock in the evening, S. Kraschnig landed a fantastic Danube salmon measuring 144cm long and weighing over 75lb! This great fish took an artificial rubber streamer lure on the stretch near Molzbichl (south of Millstatter lake). 58½lb Danube salmon have also been landed near Villach.

The upper reaches of the Drau around Lienz provide good sport, with trout and grayling up to 4½lb. The lower river winds its way close to the Yugoslavian border near Klagenfurt before crossing it at Drivograd. The whole area provides sport for many species, but I'll try to put you onto some of the best.

East of Klagenfurt on route 70 is the town of Völkermarkt. Just to the south of town the river runs into a large lake called Völkermarkter. This large stretch of water is one of the best carp lakes in Austria, with many carp over 30lb up to 47½lb.

At the eastern end, the lake flows through a long, narrow channel before opening out into another section of lake near Gurtschitschach. A fantastic looking common carp of 53lb was caught here in 1989 using raisin as bait! Many other species exist in the Völkermarkter/Drau lake system, including catfish in excess of 180lb.

Both the A2 motorway and main road west of Klagenfurt hug the coastline of the large Wärther lake near Krumpendorf on their way to Villach. This lake, and the smaller (10½km long!) Ossiacher lake to the north west at Ossiach, hold pike and carp to 35lb+, zander to 15lb+ and big cats to 100lb+, with the chance of a 200lb fish!

Seven smaller lakes lie to the south of Warther lake (Hafner, Keulschacher, Retz,Rauschele etc.) and most hold good carp, tench, pike and grass carp (to 50lb).

On route 98 north of Villach, at the towns of Scherzboden and Erlach, lie the Brenn and Afritzer lakes. These two beautiful looking waters, surrounded by hills and woodland, contain pike up to 30lb, plus good carp and cats.

The much larger Millstätter lake (further on the 98), is another good pike water, which also holds large zander and trout. The long stretch of water to the south west (at Neusach), called Weizen, is an even better proposition for big pike, with specimens to 41½lb landed!

A nice trout water lies near the German/Austrian border at Walchee (north east of Kufstein on route 175/172). The Walch lake has turned up trout to 17½lb.

The 172 road crosses the river Ache at Hütte. This river holds Danube salmon to 30lb and good chub. The impressive Boden lake has been mentioned in the German chapter, so I will just mention the Bregenzer-Ache river that runs into the eastern end of the lake, which contains nice chub up to 5½lb.

NB. A 59½lb carp (109 cms long) was caught on a boilie from Gösselsdorfer Lake in Austria in 1990.

We now cross the border into **Switzerland**. South of Zurich lie four lakes; the huge Zurich lake (chub record 5½lb), the smaller adjoining Ober lake, the Greifen lake and the smallest, the Pfaffiker lake at Pfaffikon. All hold large examples of most species, but the Pfaffiker is probably the easiest to tackle; it is a good bream water, with fish over 8lb (record 10lb) and pike to 30lb+.

To the west of Bern are a number of large lakes. The ocean-like Neunberger lake (lac de Neuchátel) and the Bieler lake both hold large catfish to 130lb, but the much smaller (but still big!) Murten Lake (lac de Morat) is, in my view, a better water. Amongst many species, the Murten holds cats to 170lb (caught in nets - the rod caught record is only 88lb), and pike to 45lb!

To the south east of Murter, the Saane river runs into the Schiffen lake. This lake contains zander to 20lb+ and tench to 8lb+. Large grayling have been caught upstream in the river Glane tributary, south of Fibourg.

The river Doubs flows along the border before bending east into Switzerland at Ursanne and then back west towards the French border. This is a very good barbel, chub, trout and grayling river. To find out more about this river, refer to the French chapter.

The river Aare between Bieler lake and the Wohlen lake near Bern holds

*Some colossal rudd, like this big specimen, have been landed from the back water of the Donou.*

pike to 30lb+, chub to 5lb+ and zander into double figures, including grayling to 3lb+ and trout over 12lb (record 12½lb) in the upper reaches, and tench to 8¾lb in the lake.

Between the Ober lake and the Walen lake at Weesen, runs the Linth canal. This canal has produced trout over 28lb and barbel over 9lb (the Swiss barbel record was caught in the upper reaches of the Rhine at 15½lb).

The Rot lake near Luzern holds carp up to 28lb+. The Wagitaler lake at Innerthal (west of Walen lake) is a good trout water, with rainbows to 9¾lb and big perch to 3½lb. The large Maggiore lake which stretches into Switzerland at Locarno is mentioned in the Italian chapter, but it's worth mentioning here that three Swiss records for 1989 were landed here, namely, powan - 5½lb, roach - 1¾lb (not so big!), and burbot - 5¾lb.

We now come back to John in the bar at St. Morritz, still trying to extract some strong liquid from a little barrel hanging from a dopey looking, big dog's neck...; if he bothers to look out of the window, he will see the upper reaches of the river Inn cutting its way through the mountains. This stretch of river has produced trout to 18½lb! The beautiful Silser, Silvaplaner and Champferer lakes on the 27 road south west of St. Moritz, all hold good trout and large char (Silser lake trout record 10½lb).

# Tour of Italy

Land of wine, women and spaghetti. This country has produced some large fish to rod and line. Here is a short list of specimens landed recently:

Carp: 59lb+., Grass carp: 32lb+., Eel: $9\frac{1}{2}$lb; Barbel: 6lb., Tench: $7\frac{1}{2}$lb; Pike: $32\frac{1}{2}$lb; Perch: $5\frac{1}{2}$lb; Zander: 17lb+., Roach: 3lb+., Trout 23lb+., Chub: $7\frac{1}{4}$lb., Catfish: $224\frac{1}{2}$lb and 275lb.

Catfish over 200lb are caught every year in Italy, but finding the true whereabouts of the lakes can be a problem. To give an example, a 275lb catfish was reported, with good photos, in both Italian and German magazines, which was caught in Lago (lake) Teaterno, but after exhaustive enquiries and research, there is no doubt that such a lake does not exist - it's not only the English who throw 'blinds' over true locations of big fish waters!

*The wonderful Alcantara cuts through volcanic rock.*

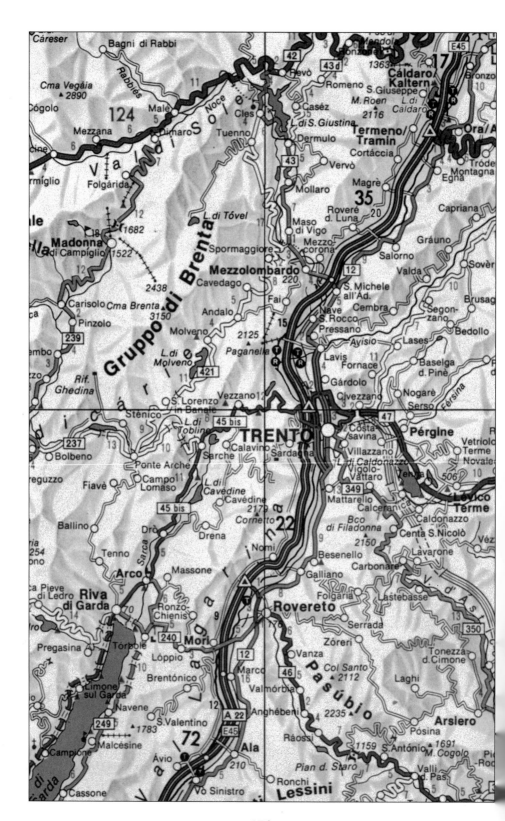

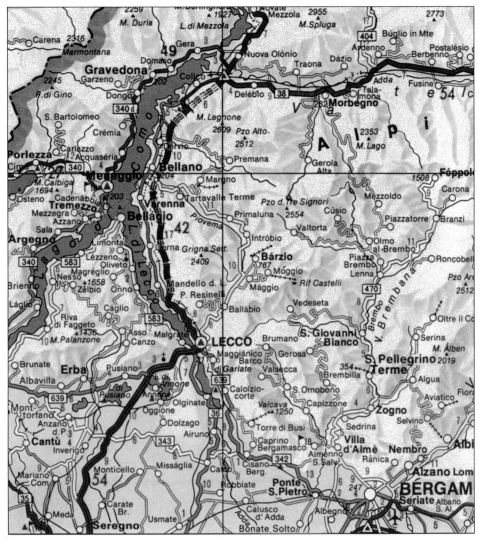

Let's do a tour from the Alps to Sicily. We begin by crossing the border at the fabulous Brenner Pass and turn off on the 43 road to Cles. Here, locked in the apple growing area of the 'Valle di Non', lies the large, St. Giustina lake, holding good trout, carp, chub, perch and eels.

If we take the small mountain road from Dermulo to Coredo, we come to the 'Duo Laghi' near Tavon. Here lie two small reservoirs which are used to irrigate the apple orchards in the surrounding area. They both hold mirror and grass carp into double figures, chub, trout and American catfish. A pleasant restaurant/bar is situated on the banks. Remember that the water level can go up and down due to the irrigation, but it is a lovely area to spend a few days in, with rocky, tree-lined gorges and high, snow-capped peaks in the background.

Turning south again, we come to Trento. There are a number of lakes holding pike, perch, tench and chub in this area, including St. Columbia, Cavedine (near Riva) and the two lakes, Canzolino and Caldonazzo on the A47 road near Pergine. The Conzolino also has a lakeside restaurant.

175

*One of the lakes at Tavon,*
*which hold good grass and*
*mirror carp.*
*Left: A good catch of carp*
*from the lakes.*

*Yugoslavia.*

*Large catfish, carp and zander in Lake Bled and the junction of the Rivers Lim and Drina at Brodar.*

*Yugoslavia.*

*Fishing from an inflatable on the reed fringed Vransko*

*A big barbel from the River Lim near Brodar.*

*A lovely pool on the River Una at Bi Hác.*

*The Plitvicka Lake system – incredible!*

*Yugoslavia.*

*Dusk on the magical Lake Bled and the upper reaches of the Sava Bohinjka River.*

The St. Massenza lake lies 18km from Trento at the foot of Mt. Gazza and contains trout, chub, carp, roach and eels. West of Trento, near Bondone, lie two lakes, Cei and Logolo, both holding carp, roach, tench, pike, trout and eels.

South of Riva on the A45 is the huge lake Garda. This 51km long water is 6km wide at the northern end and 16km wide at the southern end! It holds good trout, perch, blackbass, tench, roach, pike, eels and very large chub.

56km north of Milano at Lecco, lies the eastern arm (called Lecco lake) of the Como lake. The western arm stretches to the town of Como. This 60km long water is 5km wide and holds many large chub and good trout, perch, pike and roach.

The river Adda begins its journey from lake St. Giácomo in the 'Valle di Fraelle' (close to the Swiss border), before tumbling down through rocky passes and pools until it flows through lake Como and then on south to join the river Po. The Adda is a good chub and pike river, but trout is its real speciality, with big marmor trout to over 16lb.

The 5½km long Endine lake at Monasterolo (west of Bergamo on route 42) holds a variety of species, including big rudd to 3½lb+.

The Lugano and Maggiore lakes to the west, hold similar species as Garda. The Maggiore (64km long and 6km wide) is noted for its good tench up to 8½lb and trout to 10lb+. It also holds very big carp, but these are, of course, difficult to locate on such a large expanse of water.

The river Ticino running out of lake Maggiore, offers good trout fishing with some specimens over 10lb and pike to 20lb+. The Ticino runs into the mighty Po river. The Po provides good chub, trout and barbel fishing in the upper reaches and large pike and carp in the lower reaches. The river has to contend with a lot of pollution and if you prefer mountain clear river fishing, it is best to try the upper reaches of the tributaries, such as the Trebbia and Taro.

We now drive south west on the B45 road out of Piacenza towards Genova. The river Trebbia skirts the road all the way. This river holds good trout, chub and barbel (remember that this is the smaller Italian barbel).

North east of Torriglia, and on the eastern road out of Laccio village, lies the Brugneto lake, formed by damming a tributary of the Trebbia river. This water holds carp, tench, trout and blackbass.

Straddling the Piemone/Genova province borders, west of Busalla, we find the three Gorzente lakes, Bodana, Bruno and Lungo, all holding good trout, tench and carp.

West of the 456 road between Molare and Olba is the Orgliglieto lake near Olbicella. This lake contains nice carp, tench, eels and trout.

Driving along the A12/E1 coast road, we cross the Vara and Magra rivers (good chub/barbel fishing), until we reach Torre d. lago. North of Massa, at Vagli Sotto lies the Vagli lake, holding trout, carp and perch. Just east of Massa is the Massaciuccoli lake, a circular water with big bream, carp, eels roach and tench.

As we carry on the road east, we cross the Arno river. Upstream of Pisa there is good fishing for carp, with a number over 30lb. Further upstream at Empoli, is another good area for carp, as well as chub and bream.

North of Pisozá on the A64 at Taviano, near Porretta-terme is the lake of Suviana, holding trout, chub, pike and carp.

Upstream of St. Sofia on the river Ranco (67 road east of Firenze, then right

*Large roach and rudd are caught from Endine Lake.*

at Rocca), lies the Ridracoli, a good trout water.

We now drive south on the E6 motorway and turn off at Chiusi. Here lie the Montepulciano and the larger Chiusi lakes. North east of Chiusi on the 71 road at Castgline, is the huge Trasimano lake. All three waters hold big carp and pike, roach, chub and bream.

South west of Chiusi lies the lake St. Casciano at the town of the same name, containing trout, tench and pike.

If we drive south from Chiusi on the 71, then turn off after Ovieto on the 448 road, towards Todi, we come to the Corbara lake. This large lake is a very good carp water; the commons are very long and powerful! Best fish caught recently (1987) was a wonderful 59¼lb common!

The A71 road leaves Orvieto towards Montefiascone and then, after turning right to Bolsena, we come upon the Great Bolsena lake. This water is almost as large as Trasimano lake and holds fish of the same calibre.

Further south, through Viterbo and over point Nibbio, we come to lake Vico at Caprarola. This water holds 30lb+ carp, good tench, perch over 3lb and eels over 5lb.

South of Vico lake at Treignano, is the Bracciano lake. This lake holds large trout, chub and pike. Carp to 40lb+ inhabit the lake, but are very few in number per acre.

After driving north from Rome, on route 4, we turn off on the 578 to Fiumota. Here lies a lovely looking lake called Salto. 15km east of Salto is the Turano lake at the village of Colle di torra. Both these waters hold good carp, tench, trout, pike and perch.

Driving north east on the B4 from Rieti, we turn off on the 260 through

Amatrice, to Campatosto. Campot lake is the largest of three waters on the edge of the Gran Sasso mountains; a beautiful area to fish for good specimens of carp, tench, trout, pike, perch and eels.

Albano and the smaller Nemi lakes lie south west of Rome on the A7 road at Nemi and Albano. Both waters hold carp to 35lb+, tench, pike and eels. We now take the B6 (which follows the E45) out of Rome, then turn off on the 155 towards Fiuggi. 5km south of town lies the Cantreno lake which holds good tench, carp, pike, perch and trout, but is noted for its large eels to over $6^{1}/_{2}$lb. A nice trout water lies east of Cantreno. Take the 214/82 roads to Sora; Fibreno lake lies 10km east of Sora at the Posta Fibreno village.

Nudging the coast, south of Latina are three large lakes. Turn off the 148 road near Latina and take the coastal road towards Perco Nazionale d. Circeo. The Fogliano, Caprolace and Sabaudia lakes all hold good carp (some over 40lb, but low density per acre), tench, bream and roach. Permission can sometimes be a problem, due to this area being a reserve. Further south on the 148, just past Terraeina, is the lake Fondi; this is quite a prolific all round water, holding many different species.

A lot of good lakes lie in the Cosenza area in the south of Italy. These are the Mucone, Ariamacina, Ampollino, Arvo and Passante - all very large lakes - and the smaller lake Savuto. The best of these is the Ampollino lake, situated 12km south of St. Giovanni, near Pulumbo village. This 10km long lake lies in a beautiful area, locked in the La Sila mountains. I enjoyed a wonderful feast with friends, at a house on the banks of this water, and during the quiet evening, after a rainstorm, I caught some good trout on worms. Very large trout inhabit this tranquil lake and it also holds some large carp (to 40lb+), although these are few and far between.

The only place that I've fished in Sicily is the Alcántara river which clings to the base of the impressive Mt. Etna volcano as it tumbles and cuts its way through black volcanic rocks among majestic scenery. A first class trout river and well worth a try if you are visiting Mt. Etna. The best place to try is around Franaville di Sicila, where I caught many trout on simple Abu Droppen and Mepps spinners.

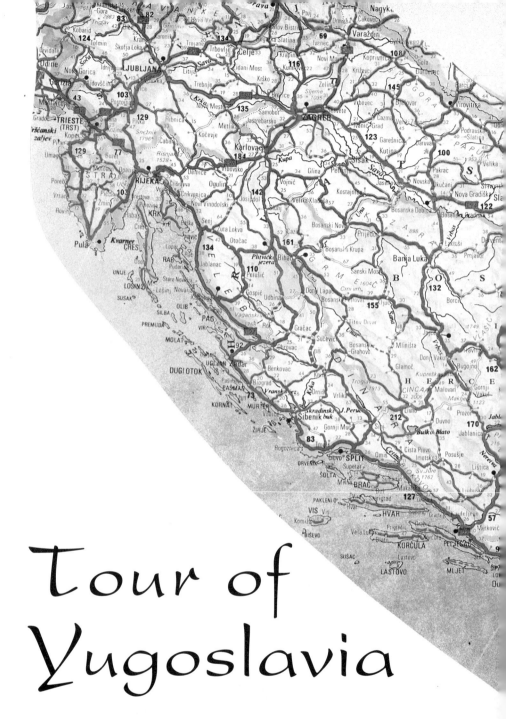

# Tour of Yugoslavia

Many people drive through Yugoslavia on the boring motorway, over the 'flatlands' via Beograd, and never taste the beauty and diversity of this wonderful country. Most of the good waters nestle among beautiful surroundings and are a must for those of you in search of wilderness areas. Yugoslavia really calls out for the wanderers amongst you - so hop on the back of my motorbike (if you dare!) as I swing through the curves on an adventure tour through the length and breadth of the country…

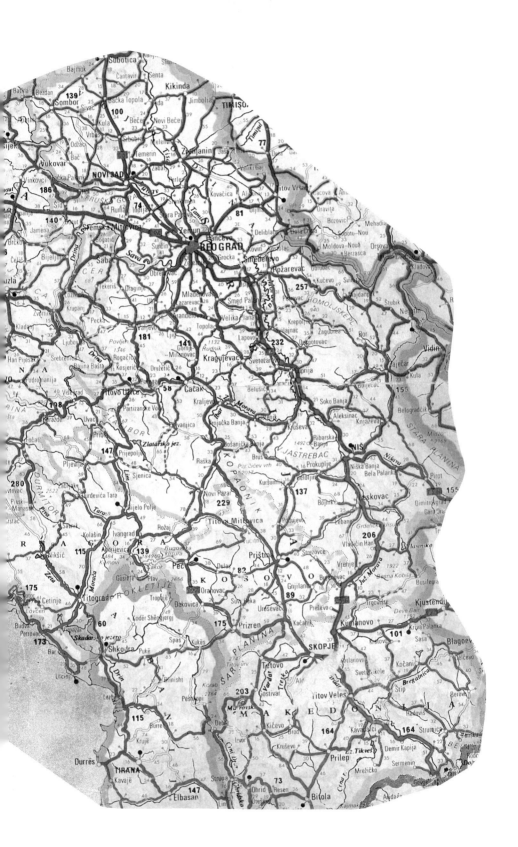

We cross over the Wurzenpass from Villach (Austria) and head towards Jesnice. (Drivers of low powered vehicles or caravans etc., should use an alternative route as this road is **very** steep with 11% gradients. The Bojbl pass has 24% gradients).

The Sava Dolinka river crosses under the road at Gord and stays with us until we reach Lesce, 12km past Jesnice. This river provides good sport with trout, chub and grayling.

4 km from Lesce is the small town of Bled. We cross over the Sava again and drive down through the swarms of tourists in Bled town, until we reach Bledsko lake. Hotels and flashy shops teeming with holiday-makers is not my idea of fun, so we drive on the road that flanks the lake until we reach the camp site situated on the south west shore, which is surrounded by towering cliffs. The sun comes out and reflects off the white, snow-capped mountains which tower over the lake; bells chime from a church on the island - one of the oldest in Europe - and a castle clings to the rocky cliffs that shadow the northern shoreline. The water is gin clear (most of the time), which makes it a good stalking water - I have even had 20lb+ carp amongst the swimmers' legs in high summer!

Species in the lake include carp (mirror, common, leather) - loads of single and double figure fish, numerous twenties, some nice 30lb+ fish and the odd 'biggie' reaching 50lb+. Grass carp up to double figures. Catfish - I have seen many cats during spawning time at close quarters and these are never fished for; sizes range from 10-70lb with the odd 100lb+ fish. Zander - some good fish with a few reaching 15lb. Tench - very few, but some reaching 10lb. Chub - many, but mainly small. Perch, roach, rudd - numerous small fish with the odd few good ones. Pike - few pike are left after many big specimens were killed by Germans and Italians in the past, but I've seen 20lb+ fish during stalking sessions.

Tickets can be bought at the hotel, club house etc., but, be warned, the cost doubles every year (one day ticket is more than a local pays for a whole year - which is a ridiculous state of affairs). Like most lakes in Yugoslavia, bivvies are out of the question and you must use the camp site or hotel.

20km from lake Bledsko lies the Bohinjsko lake at Sv. Janez. This is another glacial lake, like Bledsko, but because of its situation at higher altitude, it does not contain carp, tench or catfish. This beautiful water is fed from a waterfall that gushes from the rocks of the Kal mountain. The predominant species are trout, chub, perch (some large ones) and pike. Because of its more isolated position, this water tends to be quieter and visited less by tourists than Bled. The Sóca river on the other side of the mountain at Tomlin, is a very good area for large trout and grayling.

Back on the main road again at Lesce, we drive south to Ljubljana. The Sava Dohinka, after being swelled by many streams, now becomes the true river Sava. The Krka tributary flows down from Visnja Gora village, through Nova Masto, before joining the Sava at Brézice. The upper reaches, around N. Mesto, are good for trout, chub and grayling and the lower reaches, around Bre´zice, hold pike to 20lb+, asp to 10lb+, chub, barbel, Danube salmon to 50lb and cats to 70lb+.´

The road from Novo Mesto to Karlovac winds through lovely countryside and we cross the upper reaches of Kupa, just after Metlika. This river holds good trout, chub and pike.

The road crosses over the lovely Dobra river 5km after Netretic; a few hundred metres before the bridge on the left hand side is a cheap bed and breakfast and this is a nice place to stop for those who want to sample the chub, trout and barbel fishing of the Dobra.

The Dobra joins the Kupa at Mahicno, before flowing down through Karlovac. This town is one of the only places in Yugoslavia with a good bike mechanic who is able to screw the bike back together after it has been shaken to bits on the Yugoslavian pot-holed roads, so we stop off for a few days to sample the fishing. There are a few hotels in town and a camp site just off the E96 at Vinica on the banks of the Kupa. The Kupa itself contains good pike, chub, barbel, roach and perch and the lovely Korana holds similar fish. The Mréznica is a good trout stream.

For those of you interested in carp production, there is a large carp farm at Crna Mlaka stretching over hundreds of acres of lakes but be warned - the road to Crna Mlaka is **basic**!

Bihać (pronounced Beehach) lies 105km south of Karlovac and is a good place to base yourself. An hotel (expensive) and camp site (basic but cheap!), are situated on the banks of the river Una, just to the south of town.

It is worth visiting the Plitvicka Jezera National Park at Plitvice while you are here. This is one of the most beautiful places on earth and is a Walt Disney movie in the flesh. The Korana stream flows through a series of lakes and waterfalls amongst luxurious green foliage, flanked by towering rocky cliffs. The area is a paradise for trout fishing.

The green, and equally beautiful, Una river is a paradise of its own and must rate as one of the best rivers in Yugoslavia. Between Ostrózac and Bosanska Krupa, the river crashes through a magnificent gorge with many beautiful pools and runs. The river holds barbel to double figures, huge trout, Danube roach (maximum 5lb!) and some very large chub.

The best area for chub is around Bosanski Novi. Trout, barbel and Danube salmon can be caught between Bosanski Novi and Bosanski Krupa. There are large groups of small to medium sized barbel in the river, so you have to search for the bigger fish. One of the best areas is where the railway bridge crosses the river below Ostrózac; big barbel hold station among the old wooden bridge piles during warmer months.

Barbel can also be seen from the bridges in Bosanski Krupa, but it is strictly a 'no fishing' area (tourist attraction) as are most towns in Yugoslavia. A nice restaurant on 'stilts' towers over the river itself, just downstream of Krupa.

On the upper reaches of the Una river, at Martin Brod, near the Unac junction, is a superb area for chub, grayling and trout fishing, especially with fly or small lures.

150km south east of Bihać are the Plivsko lakes at Jajce. The Pliva river flows through two large lakes before flowing over a picturesque waterfall in Jajce town and joining the Vrbras river. The river Pliva provides good sport with trout, grayling and chub. The upper lake holds big trout (marmor type) between 10-20lb with a 50½lb 'monster' caught in 1975. The lake also holds good carp over 20lb with some over 40lb. The wooded backwaters and pools hold carp, tench and crucians.

The lower lake contains good trout, pike and carp (lake record 30lb+). A number of small, spring-fed pools lie in this vicinity - one of the best is near Loljici,

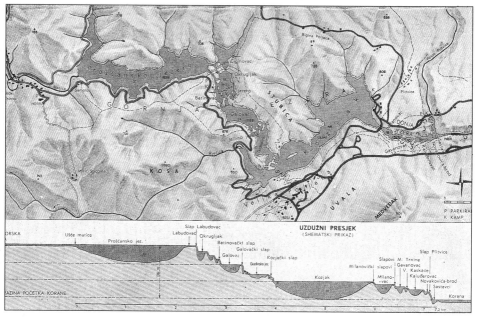

The Plitvica Lake system

The magical waters of Lake Bled.

*The wild and beautiful River Una Gorge.*

*Tony fighting a big fish in the raging waters of the Lim.*

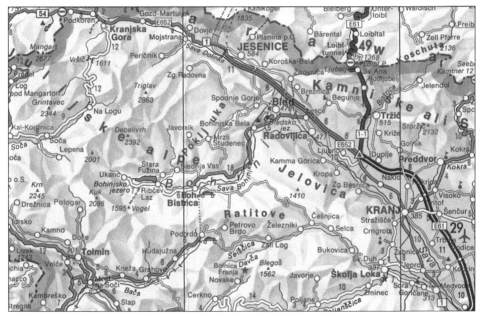

*Lake Bled, Bohinjsko Lake, Sava etc.*

with many lean, double figure fish up to 20lb+, and good tench.

The river Vrbras provides good sport with chub to 6lb, barbel up to double figures, trout to 12lb+ and the occasional big Danube salmon.

For those of you who love backpacking, I'll mention a truly wild and beautiful tributary, just north of Jajce, called the Ugar river. This river holds trout, chub and barbel and is the best tributary of the Vrbras.

We now travel south through Buojno towards Sarajevo. The large Búsko Blato and Perúcko lakes to the west, contain big carp and cats I am told, but as I have not visited these waters myself, I will leave you to find out how big!

Just after Gorica village, the Rama stream flows into the Jablanicko lake. This very long lake stretches all the way to Konjic and holds some very good fish. Anglers travel from miles around to sample the big grass carp, marmor trout, pike and chub that swim in its clear, deep waters.

The Bosna river flows north of Sarajevo and holds nice trout, chub, barbel and grayling, the best areas being around Zenca and Maglaj.

South east of Sarajevo flows the big river Drina. The Drina and its tributaries hold some enormous fish. I first read about these fish in some Yugoslavian travel books and in Anthony A. Long's 'Angeln in Europa' (translated by Wolfgang Krüger and published in 1977), and the information within those pages proved correct. A Danube salmon of over 100lb was caught here many years ago, but 10-30lb fish are more normal, with the occasional 50-70lb fish. Barbel grow to immense proportions in this river, with some monsters reaching 20lb! Chub also grow big here, with a few specimens reaching 10lb+. I have seen fish of this size with my own eyes, so there is no doubt that they exist. This does not mean that they fight to get at the first bait you throw into the water either (!), just that they exist, and like all the rivers that I know of, you must work hard to extract big fish.

186

During spring, the rivers Lim/Drina junction at Brodar is a good area for barbel. In this period the area teems with small barbel so large luncheon meat chunks, or better still, fish baits, are needed to stand any chance of a large fish. If you fish this area during the spring, you will notice that barbel are almost non existent (even the smaller fish) in the pools of the Drina opposite the junction and $\frac{1}{2}$km upstream on the Lim. Big fish only move to the Brodar junction during their spawning drive and fishing this area during summer is inadvisable as most larger fish have, by then, moved back to the deep pools of the main Drina and Tara rivers.

The best time for Danube salmon is around Christmas, during and after snow weather. In spring, when the temperature rises and the Rzav river has doubled in volume after rainfall in the mountains, huge shoals of medium sized fish move through the dam during their spawning drive, with some very large specimens amongst them. Big fish can be seen from both the dam wall and the second bridge (strictly no fishing - and a police office lies opposite!). Fishing is legal only from above the third bridge. It is noticeable how these big fish don't move within 100 metres of that third bridge. Fishermen line the Drina/Rzav junction below the dam, yet it is again noticeable that the area around the sluice gates is also strictly out of bounds - and the fish know it!

The dammed reservoir below Visegrad holds carp (some over 40lb), bream, roach, chub and catfish. The new dam above Visegrad should now be completed, so how this will affect the barbel movements remains to be seen.

The Ceotina and Tara rivers provide wonderful sport with trout, chub, barbel and Danube salmon among some of the most spectacular mountain scenery in Europe - a must for backpackers. The dam on the Komarnica is another good area.

The Krupac and Vrtac lakes near Niksic hold big carp, as does the large Bilecko lake to the west. The Klinje lake is a rocky, wild water with a lakeside hotel, and holds very big trout and a few large carp.

We now drive south west of Bilecko lake to Dubrovnik. The coastal road south takes us to the huge Skardarsko lake. The large wooded bays at the north west end provide sport with pike, eels, big cats and carp up to 40lb+.

One of Yugoslavia's best catfish lakes lies further to the north, as we head towards Sibenik on the coastal road. At Opuzen village we cross the green Neretva delta. The upper reaches of the river, south of Konjic at Glavaticevo, offers good sport with big trout. The river flows through Jablenicko lake (mentioned earlier) and then winds its way south through Mostar. This town is a popular tourist attraction; the ancient Mostar stone bridge spans the river, built in 1566 on the orders of the great Turkish conqueror, Suleyman, to replace a chain bridge deemed unsafe by his subjects. In this area, the Ottomans constructed 42 other bridges. The river flowing under this famous bridge contains good barbel, chub and trout.

Inland from Sibenik lies the Prukljansko lake. The camp site at Skradin is a good area to stay, and good fishing is to be had for numerous species upstream of Skradinski waterfall, in Visovac lake. The Krka river upstream, holds nice chub, trout and plenty of barbel, especially at Skarica, the pool at Marasovine and around Knin.

Further north on the coast road from Sibenik lies the 15km long Vransko lake. A good camp site is situated on the north western shoreline and provides good facilities, including boats (with or without outboards), for 12-24 hour hire. A boat is a must to cover this lake properly, due to the large expanse of reed beds. The lake is particularly shallow at the northern end (2-10ft) and is a good area to try. There is a large common carp population in this lake. Most of these fish are wild fish transported from Hungary during the last war and so rarely reach over 30lb - the best my friend, Peter Rünnpurge landed was 34½lb - but what incredible fighters!

The water also contains many crucians and other species, but it is the catfish that interest us most. The lake holds many cats between 30-80lb, with some over 100lb and a good chance of contacting 200-300lb fish! Landing one, among the reed beds, is another matter!! The best landed by Peter was 70lb+. Another friend, Zelko Kralj (probably the most experienced catfish angler on Vransko) has landed many cats over 100lb, up to 220lb+, but these were caught on hand lines (he still refuses to believe that the famous Cassien catfish was landed on rod and line, after the trouble he went to when landing some of his own fish!). The stories of boats dragged around the lake all day are numerous and most of the 'monster' cats are landed using heavy hand lines. After seeing a colossal cat swimming under my dinghy one morning, leaving masses of fizzing bubbles in its wake, I wondered how anything less than shark tackle could stop it in those reeds!

Most of the serious carp anglers fish tight inside the reed beds for the carp and use hook-and-hold tactics with heavy tackle. Some of them bait their swims with large feed tablets for many days. These tablets are formed by crushing hundreds of melon pips, oil and other ingredients to make a solid (and I mean solid) disc of bait about 12-16 inches in diameter, which is literally dumped in the 'marked' swim, to slowly dissolve and be 'nibbled' by the carp - quite ingenious! Boilies have yet to be used here, but they seem to accept them after a few days' baiting, so bring some basic-based hard boilies with you. Also bring some boat connections for your rods (and Optonics etc., if you intend to use them). Fishing **is** possible from the bank, but in very few places, due to the reed beds. There is a restaurant and bar on the camp site and the Adriatic sea is but a few minutes away - so the wife has no excuse...

*Yugoslavia – Skradin*

*"The campsite at Skradin is a good place to stay".*

188

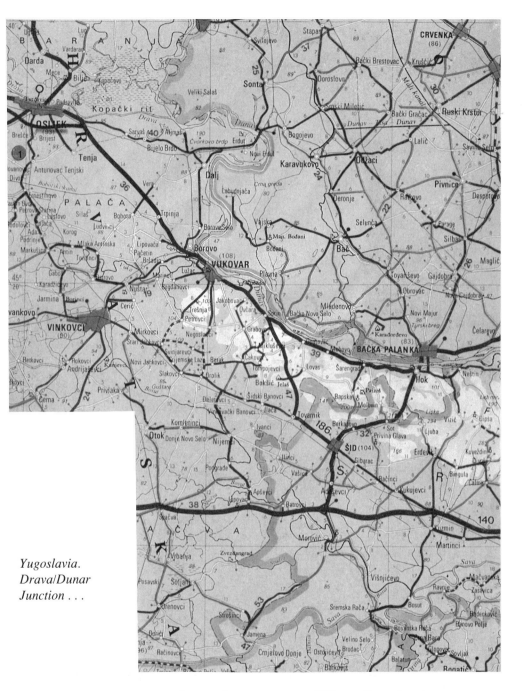

*Yugoslavia.*
*Drava/Dunar*
*Junction . . .*

We now move up to the north eastern part of Slovenija and make our way down the eastern part of Yugoslavia.

The Drau becomes the Drava as it crosses the border at Vic on its way towards Maribor. This is a good area for many different species.

Another good area lies just east of Varaždin at Šemovec where the river begins to split around many islands, and a boat is a great asset. Big carp and cats to 100lb swim in these waters and also large asp and pike.

The Soderica, an old ox-bow lake near Botovo, 16km north east of Koprivnica, is another good water for large carp, pike and cats.

Probably **the** best area on the Drava for cats lies further east at Osijek. Here the mighty Drava and Dunav rivers meet to form a labyrinth of lakes, backwaters and marshes which provide a haven for big catfish.

One of the better places lies around the village of Kopačevo (drive north from Osijek to Bilje, then take the Vardarac road for 2km before turning off right to Kopačevo). There are many cats over 100lb where the Mali Dunav enters the backwaters, with some reaching over 300lb. One of the best landed was a fantastic 13ft 6ins monster, weighing an incredible 403½lb!! Many carp swim in these backwaters, up to 40lb, with some reaching 70lb+. Other species include pike to 30lb+, asp to 20lb+ and Dunav roach to 6½lb!

Further downstream at Stari Slankamen, the large Tisa river flows into the Dunav. This river begins its long journey near Jasninja in Russia, and by the time it reaches Tokaj in Hungary, big catfish are swimming in its powerful currents. Catfish to over 400lb were caught regularly here many years ago, but 50-130lb is now more normal. Large trout, chub and barbel can be caught in the upper reaches, but by the time it reaches Kajiza in Yugoslavia it contains many different species, including carp, chub, tench, grass carp, asp, zander, cats pike, rudd, roach etc.

A good ox-bow arm lies at Curug, which joins the Veliki canal.

Another very good area lies to the north east of Titel at Belo Blato; here are numerous large lakes and pools connected by the Begej river, providing sport with many species, including big carp, cats and especially pike.

*If you want to land a record breaking monster catfish like this one try going to Osijek on the Drava River, or tho Vransko if you prefer still waters.*

The old grandfather Dunav river itself, between Apatin and Pančevo near Beograd, is broken into hundreds of arms and backwaters and holds almost every type of coarse species. I have seen photographs of some gigantic fish caught from this river, including a 10½ft long, 564lb catfish - so anything can happen when your Optonic goes off!!

The Dunav leaves Yugo at Srbovo near Negotin and becomes the Dunárea as it straddles the Rumanian/Bulgarian border, before splitting up at Glurgeni and entering the incredible Danube Delta at Galata and Tulcea. It is worth mentioning here that many big catfish were caught in the Delta during 1989-90 on rod and line (mainly by German anglers).

We now drive south of Beograd to the Zapadna river near Kraljevo. This area holds chub, pike, carp, cats etc. Large carp and cats are caught just west of Caćak at Meduvrsje.

The river Ibar enters the Morava at Kraljevo and this is a worthwhile river to fish. A lovely area lies many miles upstream in the remote mountains around Ribarice and the newly formed Gazivode and Pridvorice reservoirs. The river contains many trout, chub, barbel, grayling and a few Danube Salmon.

The Nišava river below Niš tends to become heavily polluted below the town and is better fished above Niška Banja, where nice chub, barbel and trout can be had. The large Vlassinsko lake at Vlasina, 13km east of Surdulica, is another good trout water.

The Vardar river holds carp, chub, barbel and trout with catfish in the lower reaches. Skopje is a dirty, miserable looking town and is not the best (or safest) place to stay, so try to find a place outside the town. The best areas to fish are downstream of Jegunovce village (north east of Tetova); in the Malka lake on the Treska tributary; the Crna river junction near Gadsko, and where the river splits through many islands at Gavato near the Greek border. The Crna river itself is a wonderful river which drains from the Pelagonica marshlands and then cuts through the wild, rocky mountains of the Mariovo. The best areas are around the Galiste and Tikveš lakes - a wild dirt track joins these two reservoirs between Gugakov and Kumanićevo villages.

The large, Dojransko lake to the east of Gevgelija on the Greek border, holds many species, with good stocks of carp (some reaching 40lb+). The massive Ohridsko and Prespansko lakes hold masses of fish including carp, tench, catfish, pike, roach etc., but are really too big to tackle properly unless you manage to get hold of a boat (quite a lot of netting is carried out here).

The Crni Drim river which flows into the Ohridsko lake at Struga is probably a better proposition. This river holds chub, pike, barbel, trout, carp and big eels. The best areas are the Globocica lake at Globocica village; the Spilje lake upstream near Gorenci and the large Mavroci lake, which nestles in the high Bistra-Nićpurska mountains at Mavrovi Angri.

*The Beautiful Bùlu Lake, Turkey.*

*Steve Harper strains under the weight of a magnificent 104 pound mahseer.*
*Flemming returns a 70 pounder to the rapids after an incredible fight.*

*Painted the river red and set the sky on fire.*

*Tony with a 23lb catfish caught on a fish bait.*

A big mahseer is landed after a long fight.
Johnny Jensen with an incredible 92 pound mahseer.

# Northern Greece

—

# Western Turkey

We now make our way towards one of my favourite countries - Turkey - but before we cross the border, I will mention a few waters in Greece.

In the north west corner of Greece, where it meets the borders of Albania and Yugoslavia, lies the Mikra Prespa lake at Karié. This lake holds very good carp and is probably a better proposition than the large Prespansko.

Other good carp waters in the area are, the Kastoriás lake at Kastoriá; the large Vegritas lake at Pétre and its much smaller neighbour, the Petron lake at Peréa.

The lower reaches of the Arachthos river provides good sport with average size carp, especially in the reservoir north of Arta.

The Greek catfish (silurus arislotelis), which differs very little from the Danubian catfish (except that it does not grow quite so big, rarely reaching 100lb), resides in the lower reaches of the Achelós river and surrounding lowland lakes. A good area is the Kastrakiou reservoir, north of Kastrakion village, and the Ozeros, Lissimachia and Trichonis lakes, which also hold carp. The upper reaches of the Acheleos holds good brown trout and chub.

To the east of Thessaloniki are four lakes, namely, Koronia, Volvi, Mavrúdas and Lantzas. All contain large carp, with the Volvi being the best. Just over ten years ago, a colossal carp, weighing over 90lb was caught in the nets!! Peter Rünnpurge began fishing this lake after reading reports about the capture of the monster, but now concentrates on Vransko lake because it is closer to home (besides, his wife said so!). A camp site lies on the eastern shore at Rentina and there are also camping facilities at Korinia lake.

Close to the Turkish border at Didmotichon, flows the Erithroptamus river (a tributary of the Épros), which holds barbel, chub and trout in the upper reaches, and catfish where it enters the Épros. The mighty Maritsa river (Gr: Épros, Turk: Merichnehri, Bulg: Marika) winds its muddy way along the Greek/Turkish border south of Erdine. This wide river holds many different species, including some monster cats. One experienced Greek angler who lives in Alexandroupolis, insisted that he had seen an incredible 959lb catfish caught in the nets!! This is not as far fetched a weight as it at first seems. The catfish's maximum obtainable weight is around 1,000lb and cats were caught in nets at this weight many years ago. The largest 'official' recording of a catfish was 793lb, from Russia. After

193

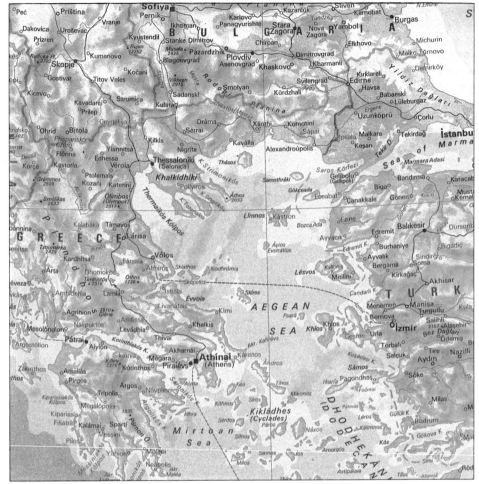

*Greece and Western Turkey.*

seeing the published photograph of a 560lb+ cat caught from the Donau, I wonder how much more ugly a 900lb+ cat could be - and how the hell would you ever stop it without an anchor?! I honestly think that 200-250lb is the limit than anyone can expect to land on the tackle normally used for large carp and cats.

Last year, I was the Managing Director of Gambia Sportfishing Ltd., and during two winters we landed on the boats many fish between 250 and 460lb, losing some even larger fish close to the boat. We were using mainly 50lb line and matching rods, yet some of the fights lasted over $3\frac{1}{2}$ hours!

The Ergene tributary is also a good catfish river, as well as holding carp, chub, bream, roach, rudd and pike.

The Gala lake to the north east of Enez holds good cats and carp (up to 30lb+).

We now cross the famous Golden Horn of Istanbul and leave Europe far behind. You only have to go a few miles off the main roads of Turkey to enter a land that hasn't changed for centuries; a land that time forgot…

*A big cat caught in static nets – Menderes river, Turkey.*
*Below: West Turkey.*

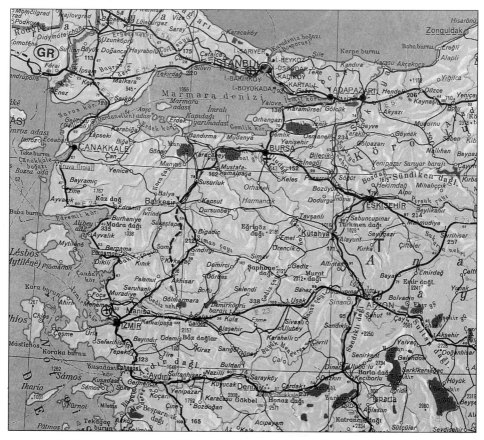

If you are driving on the main E5 route towards Ankara, it is wise to get off the dusty road for a while to have a break from the heavy lorry and goods traffic (and crazy drivers!) that pound the tarmac to bits.

Just after Düzce, the road begins to climb through some beautiful green hills of the Kirik Dag. Before the town of Bolu, turn off right and drive down the small, wooded 140 road that winds its way for 28km until it reaches a clear water lake. Abant Gölü (Gölü = lake) is a beautiful, relatively small, lake holding good pike, trout, tench, rudd, roach and a few large carp.

By driving further south through Murdurnu and Nallihan, we come to the very large Sariyar reservoir at Cayirhan. The Sariyar lake runs into the Gökcekaya reservoir which was formed by damming the Sakarya river near the mountain village of Kuyupinar. The reservoirs hold barbel, chub and large trout. The lower reaches of the Sakarya river cling to the road all the way to Osmali. There are plenty of nice areas to fish along this road (650 road, south of Adapazari), with the best at Düzakeasehir and Mekece.

The huge Kus and Uhiabat lakes to the west of Bursa contain carp over 40lb and big cats, among various other species, but a boat is really needed to cover the waters properly. The Hanife river system which runs between these two great lakes holds many species, including roach, chub, pike, carp to 40lb and catfish to 100lb+. Heavy and uncontrolled netting has caused a heavy toll on the catfish stocks on this river system in recent years. The least fished area, which still holds very big cats, is the Kara river, between Sultanyie and Karacebey.

60km south east of Balikesir near the town of Sindirgi, lies the desolate Caygoren reservoir. This wild and lonely water contains good trout and a small stock of 'big' carp. On route 525 between Söke and Milas, is the large Bafa lake, which holds some very large carp and cats.

Four much smaller, and easier to tackle, waters lie just to the north of Bafa near Karacahavit and Özbasi villages. The best of these is Azap lake. Close to these lakes flows the mighty, meandering river Menderes. This powerful, wide, muddy river holds many good barbel (mainly single figures), big carp, chub and catfish up to 200lb+. One of the best areas lies at Direcik village near Yenipazar.

*Turkey: Menderes River, Isikli Lake,*
*Bafa Lake,*
*Akcay River,*
*Azap Lake.*

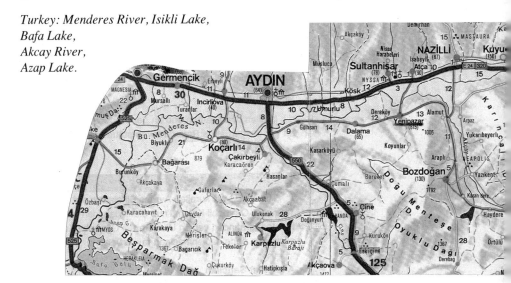

*The Isikli Lake holds some very good carp.*

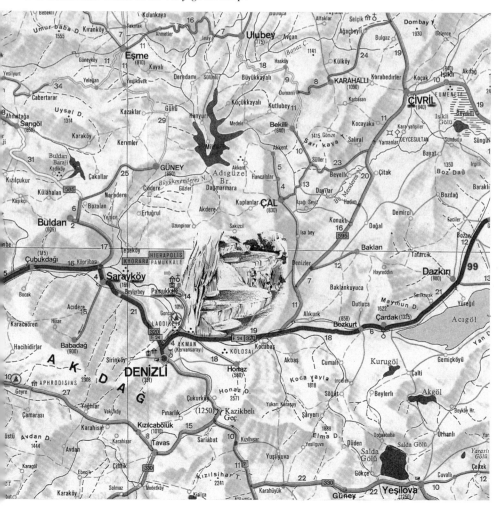

The Akcay tributary also holds good catfish and carp, and houses eels up to 10lb! The upper reaches of the Akcay provides good sport with trout, but don't go too far upstream or you'll get your head blown off by the military training in the area around Kemer!

Another good area is where the Curiksin and Menderes rivers meet, just east of Koprubasi village, near Saraykoy. Carp to 20lb+ and catfish up to $187^1/_4$lb have been caught in nets on the Curiksin river.

The upper reaches of the Mendres flow through a lovely lake, near Sundurlu village to the east of Civril (turn off the E24 from Denizili and drive north on the 595 to Civril. Take route 625 out of Civril, then turn south on a small road, after 5km). This wonderful, reed fringed lake lies in a desolate spot between the Ak and Boź mountains. It is a beautiful and timeless place to spend warm, sultry evenings, watching the wild tortoises clambering over the rocks in slow motion, while you wait for one of the big carp and catfish that inhabit this lake to take your bait. Big catfish and carp up to 50lb swim in its clear waters. There are vast reed beds on the lake and a boat is a big advantage, although there are some areas not far from the dam that can be tackled from bankside swims. The river running out of the lake provides good fishing for medium sized barbel, roach, chub, pike and carp into double figures.

Turkey is the cheapest country in this book (half the price of Greece!) and is a fantastic place to explore. Pensions are **very** low priced and tend to only rise when you enter major cities or tourist resorts. A good guide to prices, how to get there, and other facts about the country can be found in 'Turkey - A Travel Survival Kit' published by Lonely Planet publications. I have hitchhiked and camped through this country and found the people to be some of the most friendly I have ever encountered. If you expect good motorways and MacDonalds every 5 miles, don't step foot on its ancient soil, but for pure adventure and gorgeous weather, combined with cheap food and drink, look no further - and the next person who writes to me asking where he can buy bivvies and bedchairs in Turkey, I'm gonna cry...!! (That's not a joke either!).

# The Mighty Mahseer

### Johnny Jensen

*Steve Harper cradles his fantastic 104lb mahseer – the best for over 45 years.*

The Mahseer is indeed royalty in the world of sportfishing. A fish capable of making an Englishman regard the 'lordly salmon's sporting qualities as inferior, in comparison'. High praise from Mr. H. S. Thomas in the year 1873 - the Isaac Walton of Indian angling literature.

In 1903, the term 'Mighty Mahseer' appeared for the first time, incorporated in the title of a book on angling in India by a man who used the nom-de-plume 'Skeney Dhu', but even generations before this, the mahseer found its place as a highly treasured game fish, because of its superb fighting spirit.

One of the first recorded 'big ones' was caught in 1870, a 110 pounder caught on handline by G. P. Sanderson in the Cubbany river. The first mahseer to enter the book of records of fish caught on rod and reel was caught in Cauvery river near Sirangapatna in 1906 by Mr. C. E. Murray Aynsley. This mahseer weighed 104lb and a commemorative stone was reportedly erected on the bank of the river at the spot where the fish was landed.

In the following 40 years, more than 10 fish over 100lb were registered from the Cauvery-Cubbany river system. One of the most famous catches was made by Major J. S. Rivett-Carnac in 1919 in the Cauvery river. A fish weighing 119lb headed the record list for more than 25 years, when J. Dewet Van Iingen beat it by only 1lb. 120lb of sheer dynamite - a record which still stands today. Since then, there has been no record of mahseer weighing over 100lb, but the locals landed giants of 100-112lb on handline some 10 years ago.

Before the ABU team in 1978 'refound' the mighty mahseer, the fishing had declined rapidly when the British left India in 1947, but after these three fishing companions' adventurous story, French, British and Germans started invading the Cauvery and Cubbany rivers in search of this magnificent fish that had been virtually forgotten for more than 30 years.

Even though there have been no records of fish over the magic 100lb during the past 45 years, wonderful catches have been made by several eager fishermen, including my good friend, John Wilson. A very skilled, all round angler indeed, who had the unique distinction of catching a 92 pounder and an 81 pounder on the same day. Other known British sports anglers have conquered the mahseer, namely, Paul Boote with a 75 pounder; Jeremy Wade with a 95¼ pounder; John Watson with an 88 pounder and Andy Davidson with a 95 pounder and an 88 pounder. Pierre Affra also wrote (with photographs) of some big mahseer between 30 and 40 kilos caught last year.

The mahseer, being a barbel in the big family of cyprinids, is named Barbus Tor in latin. The name 'Mighty Mahseer' is not without relevance. Roughly translated, mahseer means 'great mouth' (maha meaning great, hence Maharaja), and that couldn't be more true. The protrudable, vacuum-cleaner-like mouth is a big, deep shaft ending in the impressive armour of closely packed carp teeth, enabling it to crush watersnails, crabs and shells - and, of course, most of the hardware from a fisherman's tackle box! The mouth is muscular and very powerful, the lips resembling hard rubber, and with this device the mahseer is able to kill smaller fish by sheer compression. Still, the lips are extremely sensitive, equipping the mahseer with a tool capable of picking up single rice grains, one by one, at an incredible speed; and, of course, this huge mouth, so unlike the mouth of a European carp or barbel in size, fascinates any angler, troubling him with dreams of challenging this giant in the extremely beautiful and exciting

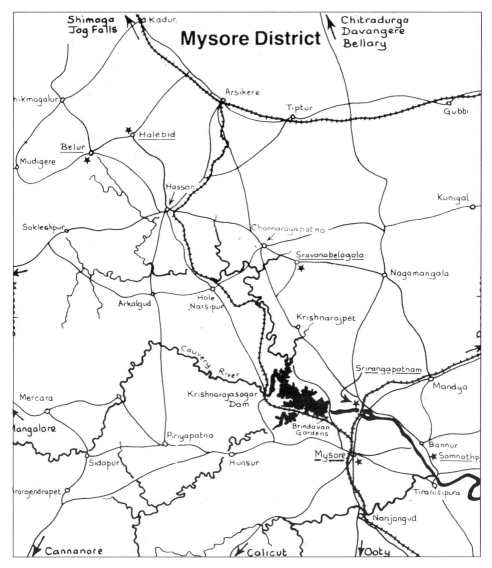

Shimoga Jog Falls ← ○ Kadur  **Mysore District**  Chitradurga Davangere Bellary

hikmagalur

Arsikere

Tiptur

Gubbi

★ Halebid

Belur

Mudigere

Hassan

Kunigal

Sakleshpur

Channarayapatna

Sravanabelogola

Nagamangala

Arkalgud

Hole Narsipur

Krishnarajpet

Cauvery River

Srirangapatnam

Mercara

Krishnarajasagar Dam

Mandya

Mangalore

Piriyapatna

Brindavan Gardens

Bannur

Somnathp.

Sidapur

Hunsur

Mysore

rarajendrapet

Tirarasipura

Nanjangud

Cannanore

Calicut

Ooty

environment of the tropical south Indian jungle.

Even though it's not difficult to get a mahseer in Cauvery at present, the fish is far from common in the Indian waters. Years of poisoning, dynamiting, netting and hydro-electric plants have put this big scaled carp on the verge of extinction. Before, the mahseer lived all over India, Burma, Hong Kong, and probably the rest of the countries surrounding India. In the river Ganges, mahseer have been seen to 150lb in 'sacred' pools of the river, and numbers of fish between 30 and 80lb+ have been taken in other areas of the river. Remember that the best periods to fish in northern India are during clear water conditions on the upper tributaries, directly after the monsoons, when the rivers start to drop rapidly again. This period can vary from year to year and in different areas, but usually lies between early and late autumn. Other good areas are the Beas river and the Corbett National Wildlife Park. The Beas has produced fish to 140lb in the past, near

201

Mandi, but due to excessive, uncontrolled netting and explosives, the river fell into decline. However, much work was put in to save the mahseer in this river from the mid-seventies onwards and the future looks brighter.

Paul Boote caught some small mahseer during the late seventies, and now in the 90's reports of big fish are again coming through on the grapevine. Close relatives of the mahseer have been caught in the two great rivers of Irak, up to 140lb in the past, but reports in recent years of big fish are hard to obtain. Tony has heard of 100lb+ fish in eastern Turkey and also reports of having seen medium sized specimens caught in the Nile. Old reports and photographs of big mahseer-like fish caught in Thailand's large rivers has also whetted both mine and Tony's appetites for new and untouched river territory, and hopefully we can plan a trip there in the future.

In southern India, the best fishing is in Cauvery and Cubbany, and from what I am told, a river south of Cauvery holds mahseer, but unfortunately I am not familiar with the area and name.

The fact that the mahseer can still be caught in Indian waters, giving anglers the fantastic thrill of pursuing and catching these monster fish, wouldn't have been possible at all if it wasn't for the hard work and determination of the Indian Wildlife organisations. They saved the mahseer just before it was too late, and are now preserving the waters and the fragile wildlife surrounding them.

The Cauvery river springs from the high mountains in Tamil Nadu, and crosses the Indian continent from west to east, passing desolate mountain areas, beautifully vegetated jungle with mangrove-like banks, inhabited by huge crocodiles. In the south Indian state of Karnataka, the Cauvery holds large numbers of mahseer in four varieties.

*Tony returns a big Indian catfish.*

Imagine fishing for mahseer, surrounded by wild elephants, stealing monkeys, poisonous spiders and scorpions, big eagles and vultures! I can't express it clearer than saying it's like fishing in a zoo, with all the animals together at the same time. Finally, the sounds and smells of the jungle to conclude the lovely picture and your irreplaceable adventure there. Waking up in the morning to the sounds and smells of the jungle is close to indescribable; your nostrils are filled with a sweet and spiced aroma and a mixed concerto of grasshoppers, eagles, monkeys monkeying around in the trees surrounding the camp, water splashing against rocks and small talk amongst the guides reaches your ears as you slowly wake up and climb out of the sleeping bag.

First thing, sitting up in bed, is Bala serving Indian tea on which I always burn my tongue. After a quick check for 'creep' in my shoes, I start packing for the morning's fishing down in the rapids, where 'the big ones' hang out. Having loaded camera, water tank, fishing gear, sun lotion and sunglasses in my bag, we start to cross the river in the little bathtub of a boat, called a coracle. From here we walk a good mile downstream, through dense jungle, over rocks and in sandy passages that are usually flooded in the rainy season.

At the pool, where we want to start fishing, we cross a small stream of furiously fast water to reach our favourite 'centre rock'. Crossing here isn't exactly walking the park, even though the guides seem to make it look easy whilst carrying all my things - camera, bag and fishing rods. Walking on these devilish, slippery stones and sharp rocks in waist high thundering water made me look like a pensioner on ice, caught in a thunderstorm! Quite a sight I gather!!

After emerging on the centre rocks, wet and dirty, I can start fishing at once, as the guides have tackled my rod during the little performance I gave on challenging the Cauvery river. On a hook size 8/0 we put a 'chilwa', a weird looking sucker fish, and a spiral lead is fixed on the line, ten inches above the bait. In faltering English, the guides start telling me about the catches from this pool and point to the best spots.

I'm casting to a promising spot, letting the heavy bait draw line off the reel as it makes its way over the rocky bottom when, all of a sudden, it gets caught down there. After tightening the line I leave the reel on open spool, holding it firmly with my thumb; and then we wait - although in the jungle, waiting isn't too hard, with all the animals around you. From time to time the fish eagles and enormous vultures pass low over our heads, hunting - if they're not lazily letting themselves get carried far, far up in the sky by warm morning thermals. These thermal bubbles often hold ten to fifteen big birds, an incredible sight. Moments like this, and hearing elephants trumpeting in the distance, hardly keep your attention fixed on the rod; but not to worry - there's nothing like a mahseer biting. Like an explosion, I'm violently ripped out of my daydreaming as the rod is close to being torn out of my hands, even though the reel is on free spool. As the line speeds out from under my thumb, I hit the handle with the other hand to lock the reel and I strike (though striking is unnecessary). My 11ft, fast action, Berkley rod bends all the way down to the handle; the line shrieks off the Ambassador 7000C reel, even though the brake is set dead hard, and I'm in the middle of playing a runaway train at full speed.

After sucking my thumb that got burned on the line during the take, I slowly and carefully descend from the rocks. In the water, I feel Subaan's hands in my back, supporting me as I stagger through the river once again, trying to get closer to the fish as it pulls line out. A grim picture occurs in my mind of how this fight might end - then the fish stops! There's only a little line left on the reel and out there it's caught around a big rock in the middle of the rushing waterfall. All I sense is the sickening feeling you experience when rocks are ripping the line.

Subaan doesn't hesitate. He quickly puts his shirt, cigarettes and cap on a rock and starts swimming out in the middle of the current. It doesn't take long before he reaches the waterfall and the rock. Climbing up, with the line in his hand, he signals me to give more line; he tries to 'whip' the line out from under the rock but the fast water keeps it fixed there. For a few seconds he seems to be deciding what to do, then he lets go of the line and tiptoes down the waterfall on a path of rocks. About 20 yards down he picks up the line on the other side of the rocks and returns to where it's stuck. Again he signals me to let out line, grabs hold of it, then - bites through the line! I can't describe how I felt, seeing him hold the line with the mahseer in one hand and my end of the line in the other - but I **can** imagine my expression of disbelief as he ties the ends back together and the fight goes on again!!

After thirty more minutes of me pumping and letting go, Subaan shovels the fish up with his arms. As the beautiful, 70lb+, golden mahseer is lifted out of the Cauvery river, gallons of water blow out of its huge mouth; a sight I will remember until the day I die.

*Fleming Jensen cradles 70 lb of mighty mahseer.*

204

As soon as Subaan got the fish under control, he ties it through its mouth with a strong nylon rope and lets it rest in the slowly running water beside us. All three of us just sit there, staring at this beautiful, gigantic fish, unable to comprehend that we actually succeeded in conquering it, suddenly realising it had taken us no less than 65 minutes.

After a while, we untie the mahseer, weigh it in a wet canvas sling and begin taking pictures with a thrill that's difficult to explain, but known to any fisherman who has caught his 'dream fish'. Fifty pictures later, we say goodbye, thanks and, hopefully, see you again next year…

Riding high from our adventure, we return to camp at noon, where Bala's got omelette and hot 'chai' ready. After eating, we prepare 'ragi' for the evening's fishing. Ragi is made of the local finger-millet, mixed with spices, usually caraway seeds, and then boiled for thirty minutes. The ragi is then easily moulded as modelling clay, which makes it a perfect bait, even on a single hook.

The evening fishing was quite uneventful, except for a few smaller mahseer, ranging from 5 to 25lb!

Sitting on the rocks, watching the sun set, elephants coming down to the waterfront for a drink and cormorants in low flight over the river, homebound after a long, hot day, I have only one thought in my mind, 'This is definitely not the last time I will see the Cauvery river!'

In fact, it was not the last time. In February 1991, Tony, Flemming and I went to the Cauvery again.

When we arrived at the river, the conditions were perfect, low and warm water, bright sunlight and a lot of fish moving. Dave Plummer, Steve Harper, John Bailey and Joy Hurst had already spent a week here when we showed up and had had plenty of fish up to about 60lb.

During the following week, history was written in the Wasi book of records. For the first time in 45 years, the 100lb barrier was broken. Steve Harper landed a beautiful golden mahseer of 106lb. Steve and Dave agreed to knock of 2lb to compensate for the water (which was non-existent) in the weigh sling. 104lb now stands as the record of the past four decades and the only recorded 100 pounder in this period.

Both Flemming and I had our personal bests at this time and Tony finally had his first mahseer. He caught a 44lb golden mahseer on a lure in the white water of Mosle Halla, which runs up to about 16 knots. He lost some monsters which stripped his baitrunners of line each time and there's no doubt he'll be back next year, challenging these legends of immense power.

The day Tony landed his 44 pounder, I had my own fight of fury. I fought a golden beast for one and a half hours through waterfalls, deep gorges and terribly powerful current. I had to swim across several times and, more than once, I went under, with only the rod tip showing above the surface. Subaan and I finally landed a stocky 92lb golden mahseer, which left us completely exhausted and washed out, but not even the thought of the hellish 16 miles journey through the jungle, on a worn out bicycle, which I had in front of me, could wash out the strength I needed to lift up my monster mahseer for about two and a half films' worth of pictures.

Flemming had a series of 30 pounders both this, and last year, so when he finally saw Subaan holding the 70lb goldie by its gills, sitting on a rock in the

*When's this going to stop!! The drama and excitement of playing a mahseer.*
*It's not only fish that bite in the Cauvery River.*

*A long and powerful mahseer from Cauvery.*

middle of the Mosle Halla rapids, he looked very victorious, but this was only until Subaan started swimming across to the bank, still holding the fish in his hands. Flemming's eyes looked as if they are about to fall out of their sockets, but as he realised the fish was reaching safety, a smile slowly appeared on his boyish face, followed by some jumping around on the rocks, shouting and screaming.

All in all, our trip was a perfect success, and a bonus was added by the catch of a 30lb black and a 16lb green mahseer. These two types of mahseer are quite rare and extremely beautiful. The black ones grow to the same size as the golden, which is the biggest, but the green mahseer seems to top around the 30lb mark. This may very well be because it is a cross breed between the mahseer and what they call 'pink carp' which, in fact, is a pink-blue barbel. This 'pink carp' doesn't grow as big as the mahseer, but some reach 40lb.

The Cauvery and the jungle around it, once again, produced fantastic fishing and some invaluably beautiful and special wild life scenes, such as panthers hunting cattle, monkeys stealing from our camp (not so funny), big and poisonous scorpions in our tents (less funny) and the breathtaking view from the mountain top over the Cauvery Valley as the sun sets on the horizon…

# India

Two people see the same scene from different angles; drink the same wine with different tastes. Johnny has given his feelings of India and here I will attempt to give the reader a view of India through my own eyes…

A deafening roar awoke me from my deep slumber. Loud cracking sounds wrenched the night stillness and wild monkeys barked their uneasiness from the branches that spread like witches' fingers above my head. A torchlight flicked on and nervously waved about like a huge dancing firefly. John Bailey held it at the source and apprehensively asked the guides whether they were soon to be trampled to death.

"Turn out the torch, Boss", Bula whispered. "Or else the elephants will charge if you blind them with the light".

Just at that moment an even louder 'roarrRRR' echoed from within the bowels of a big bull elephant, but a few hundred metres distant. The torchlight suddenly vanished and I could hear John's uneasy, irregular breathing as he listened to the elephants ripping trees from the soil and breaking the heavy branches with loud cracking sounds as they came closer and closer to the camp.

A deep, grinding, rumbling sound, like heavy rocks being rubbed together, started to echo from one of the tents and I jerked my head from the pillow, expecting any minute to see Dave Plummer's tent trampled underfoot. No huge elephant trunk materialised from his tent, however, and it slowly dawned on me that it was just Dave's own nostrils inflating to the noisy irregular intakes of breath, while he was locked in the land of dreams and monster fish.

I lay my head back down and the noisés of the trampling elephants, screeching monkeys, Dave's snoring and the guides talking by the flickering firelight, all somehow mingled into one muffled sound as I drifted into fitful sleep.

It seemed that only moments had passed before the cook entered my tent with two early morning cups of 'chi'. On opening my eyelids, I was startled awake by two eyeballs hanging upside down from the ceiling of the tent; I moved my hand up to reach them and they suddenly disappeared as the chameleon scampered to the other side of the canvas. By now, Johnny was awake, slurping, then wincing as he burnt his tongue on the hot coffee. Saban was outside the tent puffing and panting, for this morning he would be taking Johnny many miles downstream over rough jungle tracks to reach an, as yet, untouched stretch of river, but first he had to pump up the tyres on the two ancient bicycles that looked like relics from the British raj.

The tent suddenly went dark and I thought it was an eclipse, but it was just Dave walking past carrying two rods, ten bags and three kitchen sinks on his way to the river. Before he got there, however, he gave Bula all his gear except his sunglasses, then followed him lightfooted to the waiting coracle. I could hear Bula creaking and straining under the weight as he quietly talked to Dave.

"Big elephants last night, boss", and Dave replying,

"What elephants?"

Flemming was joining me this morning to have a go at plugging on the middle rapids. Murry was to be our guide so we followed in his footsteps along the jungle track as the morning sun soaked the landscape in orange light.

We eventually arrived at a pool below a stretch of violent rapids. Ragi paste and small deadbaits had been our main tactics in this area over the past few days, with no success, so we were about to try big plugs in the fast water. Flemming was a lover of rods which gave back a tremendous feel to the angler and so had chosen similar tackle to my own. We both had with us **very** progressive downrigger rods of 8-8½ft and rated to hold 12-25lb test lines. However, we were both using Berkley Big Game line rated at 40lb b.s. which was needed to combat the masses of rocks and boulders that infested this complete stretch of river. The very short butts on the downrigger rods allowed us both to use butt-pads (small fighting belts) for fighting the fish. (For casting heavy fish baits and ragi paste I also used a more powerful downrigger rod of 9ft in the 12-30lb line class).

Flemming had the first strike with a beautiful carnatic carp which fell to a silver rapala-like plug. After watching Flemming's silver scaled carp swim strongly from his hands, I was off like a jack-rabbit to the next set of rapids to have my share of the action.

I chose a very big, strong actioned American plug and cast it into an eddy that formed at the edge of the raging white water. Almost immediately the rod was wrenched over and I was into a powerful fish. Ten yards of line were quickly stripped off the reel and the fish lodged itself behind a rock. I quickly moved downsteam and, with side pressure, managed to dislodge it. Again, the line screeched off the ratchet but, within seconds, it was behind another large rock. This time the fish had placed the rock between itself and me, so no amount of pressure would budge it. The line twanged and whistled against the immense force of water and I could occasionally feel the fish pull out a yard of line then fall back behind the rock again. Each time it did so, my mind's eye could see the line being shred to pieces.

I moved 30 metres upstream to try to dislodge the line, but the incredible force of water just kept the line jammed like a magnet against the rock. Murry tried to tell me something, but I could hardly hear his voice under the deafening roar of white water. He started to swing his arm in the direction of the other side and I suddenly realised that he wanted us both to swim across. I looked down at my heavy snowboots, then back at the rapids and had terrible visions of me being sucked under, never to be seen again, until my boots popped back to the surface half a mile downstream. I slowly started to wade up to my waist, then my chest, at the edge of the powerful current, but Murry waved me back and made it clear that he wanted me to stay on this side while he alone swam over to try to dislodge the line. I hid a little smile of relief and waded back to dry land, then wedged my boots firmly on terra-firma.

*A beautiful pink barbel caught on ragi paste and light tackle.*

A white, turbanned head bobbed in the current and was swept like a leaf through the raging white water and it was not until Murry had been swept well downstream that his strong overhand strokes managed to pull him out of the flow and he eventually dragged his dripping body onto the smooth boulders of the far bank.

I moved well upstream again until Murry was able to grab the line and move back to the submerged rock then, with gently plucking, he managed to free the line. The rod felt alive again in my hands and I pressured the fish back into the current, but there was no way that I would be able to pull the great weight of the fish through that sort of current. As soon as the fish hit the full force of the flow, I let it be swept downstream towards a quieter pool of water 50 metres below. Following the fish was a nightmare and I stumbled like a cat on ice through the raging water and slippery rocks.

Flemming was, by now, standing on a promontory above the pool, watching the action with interest. I looked up at Fleming just as my left boot was planted on top of a huge, slimy, flat-faced rock. The fish chose that moment to power off on a long run as its tail gripped the beginning of the slacker water. As the rod wrenched round, I planted my right foot down to get a better grip. With both feet now firmly planted on the rock and the fish moving off at warp 10, it just needed the fast flowing water to sweep me straight off my feet. I went down like a Canadian tree trunk and slid along the rock on my backside, then was swept downstream like a cork before I managed to get upright again. I dragged my dripping body onto a sandbank and continued the fight, with Flemming trying to suppress his shrieks of laughter.

The rod was now bending in an incredible arc, right down to the butt pad and it was not long before a beautiful golden mahseer surfaced in the current. The supple, but progressively powerful rod, matched with a Shimano 4500 was working like a dream and I could feel every movement of the fish's body. Murry swam back across and waded out to the fish then, with a gentle underarm grip, lifted the lump of silver scales out of the water.

Little did we know that, during my fight, another battle was raging many miles downsteam, between Johnny and a huge fish weighing more than twice the weight of the mahseer I had just landed. A submerged submarine had taken a liking to Johnny's big ball of ragi paste and had stripped off nearly all the 40lb yellow Stren on his Shimano multiplier. The river crashed through a series of rapids and rocky gorges at this point and both Johnny and Saban were forced to cross the turbulent waters many times. It was not until 1½ hours later, that a tired Saban lifted a colossal 92lb humpbacked mahseer out of the raging currents. But Saban's and Johnny's ordeals were not yet over, for they still had to cycle all those miles back to camp over rocky tracks in the midday, stifling heat - with flat tyres!

India; a land of contrasts. Here we were, in a landscape devoid of humans, in a land bursting at the seams with people; fishing in a clear river, brimful of fish in a land of polluted, stinking rivers that flowed like bubbling black oil; cities full of teeming cars and humans, and jungles full of teeming wildlife with not a single human or vehicle in sight.

This was also to be a fishing trip of contrasts. I was to fall to the biggest series of bad luck that I've experienced in such a short period. Not only was I to lose three massive mahseer, but I was also to be plagued by mishap after mishap during my entire journey to and from India - more mishaps than I'd encountered in the previous 10 years of travel! But to contrast all this, I was to absorb the wonders around me, the great companionship and friendship of wonderful people like Flemming, Johnny, Dave, Joy, John, Steve and the warm hearted, hard working guides. The fantastic array of 'life' that surrounded us 24 hours a day; from scaly crocs with mouths full of teeth under the water, to scorpions and hairy spiders under the bed; from leopards chasing cows up the mountainside to cooks chasing thieving monkeys up the trees; from watching Steve's face light up when he lifted 104lb of beautiful golden mahseer above the water, to watching the line fall slack after 200 metres of 40lb line had been ripped off my reel; from the madness of Bombay city centre, to the quiet solitude of the last day in the jungle and both Bula and I sat talking quietly of the size of the monsters swimming underneath our rod tops, while the slow sinking sun painted the river red and set the sky on fire.

Memories are held for ever.